Crosscurrents / MODERN CRITIQUES

Harry T. Moore, *General Editor*

The Existentialism of
ALBERTO MORAVIA

Joan Ross *and* Donald Freed

WITH A PREFACE BY
Harry T. Moore

SOUTHERN ILLINOIS UNIVERSITY PRESS
Carbondale and *Edwardsville*

FEFFER & SIMONS, INC.
London and Amsterdam

Copyright © 1972 by Southern Illinois University Press
All rights reserved
Printed in the United States of America
Designed by Andor Braun
International Standard Book Number 0–8093–0548–8
Library of Congress Catalog Card Number 70–180628

For
Donald Kalish: The Philosopher, The Man

Contents

Preface

Alberto Moravia is one of the great novelists of our world. Hence this extremely valuable study of existentialism in his work, by Joan Ross and Donald Freed, is a most welcome addition to the Crosscurrents/Modern Critiques series.

The authors of the present book continually show how Moravia's work is intrinsically existentialist: his people must work out their own destiny, in novel after novel, story after story.

We have not so far had, in English, so thorough an examination of the man and his meaning, for the authors show, as no one else has in our language, how closely Moravia's work is linked to nature, and how he deals with natural symbols.

Philip Rahv once noted, in an introduction to a volume of this author's short stories, that "the craftsman in Moravia is fully aware of the opportunities offered by each scene, act, and movement of the psyche," and the authors of the present book develop such ideas at length, for they deal not only with the philosophy of Moravia—one of the most intellectual and best read of modern fiction writers—but also with him as a craftsman.

We are all grateful for Moravia's novels such as The Time of Indifference, The Conformist, and The Woman of Rome, to name only three of the best known, and for such short stories as "Bitter Honeymoon," with its vital account of the girl Communist (a blonde Italian who can recite Dante) who marries a nonpolitical man and goes with him for a honeymoon on Capri (actually Anacapri): here the existential theme is worked out marvelously and the natural symbolism (the small lake, the lightning) intensifies the basic situation.

Fortunately, Moravia's work is widely obtainable in the United States, both in hardbound and paperback books, so that readers who, after going through the Ross-Freed book, want to become further acquainted with Moravia's work, can easily do so. And this volume, with its generous quotations from him illuminating their own comments, is the finest possible guide for such readers.

HARRY T. MOORE

Southern Illinois University
December 21, 1971

Acknowledgments

The authors wish to thank the following publishers for permission to use quotations from their books:

Reprinted with the permission of Farrar Straus & Giroux, Inc. and Martin Secker & Warburg, Ltd. from *Bitter Honeymoon and Other Stories* by Alberto Moravia, Copyright © 1956 by Valentino Bompiani & Co.

Reprinted with the permission of Farrar, Straus & Giroux, Inc. and Martin Secker & Warburg, Ltd. from *The Conformist* by Alberto Moravia, Copyright 1951 by Valentino Bompiani & Co.

Reprinted with the permission of Farrar, Straus & Giroux, Inc. and Martin Secker & Warburg, Ltd. from *Conjugal Love* by Alberto Moravia, Copyright 1951 by Valentino Bompiani & Co.

Reprinted with the permission of Farrar, Straus & Giroux, Inc. and Martin Secker & Warburg, Ltd. from *The Empty Canvas* by Alberto Moravia, Copyright © 1961 by Valentino Bompiani & Co.

Reprinted with the permission of Farrar, Straus & Giroux, Inc. and Martin Secker & Warburg, Ltd. from *The Fetish and Other Stories* by Alberto Moravia, English translation copyright © 1964 by Martin Secker & Warburg, Ltd. From *L'Automa*, copyright © 1963 by Casa Editrice Valentino Bompiani.

Reprinted with the permission of Farrar, Straus & Giroux, Inc. and Martin Secker & Warburg, Ltd. from *The Lie* by Alberto Moravia, Copyright © 1966 by Casa Ed. Valentino Bompiani. Published in Italian under the title *L'Attenzione*, copyright © 1965 Casa Ed. Valentino Bompiani, Milan.

Reprinted with the permission of Farrar, Straus & Giroux, Inc. and Martin Secker & Warburg, Ltd. from *Man as an End* by Alberto Moravia, English translation copyright © 1965 by Martin Secker & Warburg, Limited. Published in Italian under the title *L'uomo come fine a altri saggi* © 1964 Casa Editrice Valentio Bompiani.

Reprinted with the permission of Farrar, Straus & Giroux, Inc. and Martin Secker & Warburg, Ltd. from *More Roman Tales* by Alberto Moravia, Copyright © 1963 by Martin Secker & Warburg, Ltd. Published in Italian as *Nuovi Racconti Romani,* copyright © 1959 by Valentino Bompiani & Co.

Reprinted with the permission of Farrar, Straus & Giroux, Inc. and Martin Secker & Warburg, Ltd. from *The Red Book and the Great Wall* by Alberto Moravia, Copyright © 1968 by Farrar, Straus & Giroux.

Reprinted with the permission of Farrar, Straus & Giroux, Inc. and Martin Secker & Warburg, Ltd. from *Roman Tales* by Alberto Moravia, Copyright © 1956 by Valentino Bompiani & Co.

Reprinted with the permission of Farrar, Straus & Giroux, Inc. and Martin Secker & Warburg, Ltd. from *The Time of Indifference* by Alberto Moravia, Copyright © 1953 by Valentino Bompiani & Co.

Reprinted with the permission of Farrar, Straus & Giroux, Inc. and Martin Secker & Warburg, Ltd. from *Two Adolescents* by Alberto Moravia, Copyright 1950 by Valentino Bompiani & Co., S. A.

Reprinted with the permission of Farrar, Straus & Giroux, Inc. and Martin Secker & Warburg, Ltd. from *Two Women* by Alberto Moravia, Copyright 1949 by Valentino Bompiani & Co., S. A.

Reprinted with the permission of Farrar, Straus & Giroux, Inc. and Martin Secker & Warburg, Ltd. from *The Wayward Wife and Other Stories* by Alberto Moravia, English translation copyright © 1960 by Martin Secker & Warburg, Ltd.

Reprinted with the permission of Farrar, Straus & Giroux, Inc. and Martin Secker & Warburg, Ltd. from *Woman of*

Rome by Alberto Moravia, Copyright 1949, by Valentino Bompiani & Co., S. A.

Reprinted with the permission of Random House, Inc. and Martin Secker & Warburg, Ltd. from *Confessions of Zeno* by Italo Svevo, Copyright, 1930, and renewed, 1938, by Alfred A. Knopf, Inc.

Reprinted by permission of New Directions Publishing Corporation and Martin Secker & Warburg, Ltd., from Italo Svevo, *As a Man Grows Older*, translated by Beryl de Zoete. All rights reserved.

Reprinted by permission of Oliver and Boyd, from *Moravia* by Guliano Dega.

The authors wish to thank the following individuals for their help in connection with this book. Special thanks is extended to Professor Louis Tenenbaum, Chairman of the Department of Italian, University of Colorado, for his perceptive criticism that has been both valuable and helpful. Professor Giose Rimanelli, State University of New York at Albany, deserves acknowledgment for his encouragement and support.

Appreciation for the long, arduous task of editing goes to Miss Elizabeth Wenning and Miss Frances Haley. Thanks is also extended to Miss Kathy Polk and Miss Susan Stone who gave their help to the index.

The Existentialism of Alberto Moravia

1

The Argument

"There is no such thing as *was*—only is. If *was* existed there would be no grief or sorrow." [1] Faulkner's reading, with our italics of emphasis, of the vicissitudes of memory, is magisterial. Memory makes men sick, repression of memory makes men sick, yet, to be well, the sufferer must remember both more and less. This is his psychotherapy. It is, perhaps, appropriate to begin the discussion of Alberto Moravia with a series of related paradoxes. *Psyche* is Greek for soul and *therapy* a synonym for healing. Help for the soul is the aim of everything religious, and art has a sacred source.

In some primitive clans, when a child is born a wooden image is buried in a certain place. This is the *chiringa*, the soul; the *chiringa* that will always be there as a fixed locus of identity surrounded and guaranteed by the earth itself. That is the genesis of the religious identity (*religio* in the sense of tieing back) that is rooted in earth and soul. Now men are deracinated, denatured, uprooted forever, their souls floating and blown about in the endless wind of history, and any "cure" that cannot minister to this irremediable hurt is nothing more than a straw in that wind. So the soul looks endlessly for its *chiringa*. "Where can I find my home?" asks Nietzsche on his mantic wanderings. Now, we all ask that.

One of our failed strategies is, always and everywhere, nostalgia (from *nostos*, home-going). But we cannot go home for two reasons. W*as* does not exist anymore, nor did it ever exist as we *choose* to remember it. In fact, we construct this former home out of our own awareness of loss and nothingness, or we project it forward into a heaven. It is *is*, the verb of existence, that Alberto Moravia writes with—and the parameters of his literary structure are deep and timely. "One day is enough" might have been a motto that Moravia had borrowed from one of his mentors, Dostoyevsky. But these big themes of time and inner space flow down this century from a matrix that includes psychoanalysis, existentialism, and scientific philosophy, however hard they try to be opposites of each other. After Freud the unconscious equalled timelessness. One day is enough if only the body could be cauterized of all its secret calls. Moravia, as literary healer, takes up this nostalgia of the body for its past endlessly as do all the existential men of literature. His instinct is very sound, for he senses or knows something central about what we call memory.

What are the laws and logic, as Camus called them, of the body? When Freud spoke of the "I" (ego) he spoke, he said, of the "body I," while Moravia and the others, for their part, seem to be writing of the body's memory. What else could they mean; certainly there is no such thing as the memory's memory! What but the body can be meant, for what but the body could be the instrumentality of that all-embracing impulse to go home? The body craves again those never-to-be-recaptured caresses and states of childhood, but it also translates into fantasy and projection its abnegations and renunciations. This hidden agenda of yearning and gratification of the flesh is bound to be represented by images, by the feeling of nostalgia, and finally by rebellion. This rebellion, at the deepest level, is the existential artist's field of inquiry. He is pursuing the I, or rather the structure of the I and its relation to Being. Being is comprised of energy in a certain structure called the I. The ideals, projections and sublimations, and atavisms acted out by literary models are the residue of past choices and abnegations. The energy of the "It" (id), the structure of the I, and their always-shifting interrelationship—this is the stuff of Being. The contrariety between the body and its memories (both real and regretted) produces a series of images from which the I selects its memories. The memory is the *chiringa;* unalterable, sanctified history. Looked at in this way, the neurosis is indeed a sacred idiosyncratic religion not to be given up on pain of damnation. It is to this grieving body with its deluded history that the Roman and the other twentieth-century helpers come to make an onslaught on nostalgia, to rescue *personhood* from *personality*, to replace *hiddenness* with *standing open* and being able to *stand it* (to use some of Heidegger's terms that are, for once, clear). This is the new Latin of the existential diagnosis.

Thus, soul-help means body-help in the most generous sense of the term. And the literary physician strives after that seamless web of meaning of the nonliterate aborigine for whom anything not of the here and now is called "in the dreaming." The I stands on the ruins of its choices; the I's choices are chosen from available options; these options are the upshot of biology and the nature of the world. This agenda can lead but to alienation of the It and the I, if the vital current is broken or no *chiringa* is available. The anodyne for alienation has been, in recent cultures, ratiocination and romanticism: the negative and the positive faces of nostalgia. Nietzsche marked the end of these placebos; it was they, not God, that he cancelled. We love and die now within biology and history—the very style of our existence produced by the holy war between these two inexorable forces. Neither God nor Reason may mediate from outside. The Dictionary and the Bible are vacated mythologies.

To live in a postatheistic as well as a post-Christian period is to nurture continual anxiety. The idea of Reason or of God must now be freshly invented by Camus and the others. As Buber or Kazantzakis might put it, it is they, Reason and God, who need us! Moravia's protagonists, then, are really gradations of the I, the anomalous flesh caught in its Procrustean tautology: the more one feels life calling in the *sorties* of the *soma*, the more audacious must the project, the *engagement* become; lest, under the unremitting pressures of finitude, one fall prey to memory, to *nostos*, to that hated "hope" from which the Greeks ran. For Moravia, most of the restoration will come from men and women who will help each other, after they both have realized that they are bound not only by the body's needs, but, more powerfully, by its losses and its remorse and its existential, tragic eudaemonism (that joy which, unlike euphoria, is serious and often tragic).

Now come Moravia, Camus, Sartre, and the others to pick up the pieces of the shattered towers of reason. Moravia does not need to wander looking for a home; he can sit predictably each day at his antique desk (a minor concession) and minister to his patients as they turn their corners into the present. He would have them live through their bodies and in them as if that same body were the long-sought home. That, we shall see, is the last meaning of existential literature: finitude is home, and the damned, our *Perduta Gente*, are reprieved; the *chiringa* is buried in the bones. If Moravia makes a testament of the body, it is in order to bring on a kind of good news from the nervous system.

"The dominating theme of my work seems to be that

of the relationship between man and reality." [2] And again, "Man found himself suddenly incapable of establishing a relationship with his own world, for the world had become dark and unplumbable or—worse still—it had disappeared." [3] Thus, Alberto Moravia sketches the boundaries of his world. And this essay argues that the world and work of Alberto Moravia are an important version of what is becoming the most significant vision of reality in the twentieth century: existentialism.

It cannot matter much that he might disclaim this still-evolving ideology, for as Sartre says, "Existentialism as a term no longer has any meaning." [4] We must use our words as we find them, though every movement has tried in vain to escape from a popular rendition of its terminology. It is the latest phase of this ubiquitous, and in many ways literary, philosophy that characterizes Moravia best. Not Kierkegaard, Dostoyevsky, nor Nietzsche, but the second literary generation of Sartre and Camus and Kazantzakis, are Moravia's brothers. Moravia is perhaps the best control of all for judging how deep this new world view has penetrated, since he is both unselfconscious and often unconscious of the philosophical burden he bears.

"The world . . . had disappeared," that is the best clue. If existentialism agrees on anything (and it does) it is that man, as we thought we knew him, has disappeared. It is man that makes a hole in reality when his traditional values and identity have been abrogated. When "moral man" disappears or is wiped out by great events, then the atavist surviving projects his sense of nothingness onto reality and claims that it has vanished or become a hopeless jumble of meaninglessness.

Moravia, together with Camus and Sartre, received shocks of several kinds from the war. His cosmopolitan, physically secure pattern of living became overnight a complete anomaly. A putative social critic, he was forced to flee Rome and the Fascists, not underground as his French colleagues, not into politics, but into exile, into the primitive Italian mountains. In this moral fastness he lived with the poorest of the poor, and his body of work since those days is never untouched—disguised in a hundred ways though it is—by that season of danger. While Camus and Sartre were undergoing a terrific process of socialization underground and an initiation into the imperatives of realpolitik, Moravia was cut off from the world of men and ideas and cast into the land of his imagination. While the Frenchmen were falling into history, the Italian was diving into the subjective consciousness of which he would make so much literature. Moravia, in the country, cut off from men; and the other two, underground, cut off from nature—between them they exhaust the deprivations of exile. Curious that the Italian should make a twentieth-century pantheism into a personal therapy and literary credo, like Camus, while choosing the city as his *genius loci* and obsession, like Sartre.

What was the net effect of this received trauma on the intellectuals and artists, the reaction to great crime and unremitting danger? It did many things to the morally sensitive and imaginatively strong; but above all it caused these young men to doubt their inherited reality; it humiliated them; it exploded their bright, Enlightenment megalomania; and through the gaping holes in their public personalities rushed the accumulated, palpable nothingness of this century. Thus, they had to begin over, to swim upstream in an unequal struggle whose exhaustions have fired their style with authenticity.

One of the chief purposes of this study is to insist on Alberto Moravia's right to inclusion in the pantheon of twentieth-century authenticity. His, by now large body of work, written at the interface of the convulsions of our time, mark him as one of those "good Europeans" that Nietzsche spied coming down the road of the future. But he is always an "author" (his attempts at philosophy appear rather clumsy, lacking his usual style and purity of syntax), and this seems somehow puny in a day when the air is filled with the metaphysics of armed intellectuals, when the death camp supplants the Crystal Palace as the symbol of the epoch. So let our angle of refraction be the *literature* of existentialism, and let our subject of study be the voice of Alberto Moravia, whose persuasiveness grows story by story and book by book, in the old way of the creative writer.

"The relationship between man and reality"—how ordinary this rubric has become to our failing hearing. For the fathers of existentialism in Russia, Denmark, and Germany, the agon or reconciliation was, as of old, between man and God; and the stakes, as always, were deicide and rebirth. For the existentialist epigone, the second generation, however, the affair is between men. Moravia operates quite automatically in this context that would have scandalized the truth seekers of the past and still disturbs the middle thinkers of the present moment. This "reality" that obsesses Moravia, as it does his philosophical contemporaries, is no set of Platonic images or Newtonian counters or anything else that has been offered as a coherent abstraction of reality. This reality is, to these firstlings of the twentieth century, "dark and unplumbable," but it is their native element; they write from inside it, their striving is within and between the psyche and the world, and there are no gods from the machine to round off the tragic edges of the human situation they speak of, save death and sexuality. This Mass for our century which Moravia celebrates, and which this book hopes to punctuate, is given its most downright version by the author of that doomsday book of the everyday, *Being and Nothingness*.

Freedom in its foundation coincides with the nothingness which is at the heart of man. Human-reality is free because it *is not enough*. It is free because it is perpetually wrenched away from itself and because it has been separated by a nothingness from what it is and from what it will be. . . . Man is free because he is not himself but presence to himself. The being which is what it is can not be free. Freedom is precisely the nothingness which *is made-to-be* at the heart of man and which forces human-reality *to make itself* instead of *to be* . . . Freedom is not *a* being; it is *the being* of man—i.e., his nothingness of being.[5]

This is the obligatory and most spectacular of all deductions: man is wholly and forever free. Camus sees "an absurd world where even the moles dare to hope." These sentiments, which have infected Moravia so deeply, are very much later in the day than the announcement of the death of God. That announcement is a *donnée* for Moravia and is not primary. The wound in the idea of the conscience and of the world caused by the death of the idea of God has been suppurating now for three generations. The therapy of Moravia and the other reluctant physician-patients is to begin to make a better life out of the desolation of the wound itself; to be content with nothing and to leave behind them the red footprints of their freedom. So the idea of atheism as a consolation is as irrelevant now as the idea of God was then. Atheism is simply the name of a fatal disease; and Moravia, the doctor of the autosphere, of the "dark and unplumbable" unconscious, sits elegant, lean, and lucid each day at his writing desk and, in that spare and sensuous style on which we have come to depend, strokes the bench marks of our century-end dialectic between man and reality.

In many ways Italy is the quintessential country of

alienation. Children of the Madonna and of Marx were caught in a savage civil war, only to be "rescued" by *Il Duce*. As late as 1900 there was a "legal" and a "real" Italy. The legal parliament and church ruled elite over the real masses (an electorate forbidden by the Pope to vote!). Impotence was called grace. Liberalism was impotent, masochistic, moving toward fascism.

In this land of no holding center, Moravia beats his retreat into the body, there to make his stronghold. His politics are actually philosophy. He is a "Left" existentialist on the verge of dialectical materialism, but finally, midway between Camus's silence and Sartre's scream.

It is this same philosophically radical angle of refraction that sponsors his revealing comments on China and America. His American complaint is unusual in that the charge that she has lost her soul assumes that she has had one, but his China speculation is extraordinary. The historioanalysis of China gives us by indirection her tragic estimation of the West. Western man is born violent, drenched in blood and sex, and Christianity only seals his fate in guilt which in turn leads on to more crime.

> Even in moments of the greatest violence, private or public, the Chinese fail to reach the primitive violence of their original nature beneath the second nature they have acquired through culture. In the West, on the other hand, culture is much more recent, nothing more than a veil thrown over a primordial violence that is always ready to explode. Thus, whereas the Westerner never finds it very difficult to regress in an instant to Neanderthal man (as we saw during World War II), the Chinese despite his efforts, remains the man of the T'ang dynasty. A curious consequence follows from this: Western man is born violent and dedicates his whole life to learning to be

cultivated and civil. The Chinese, on the other hand, is born cultivated and civil and must learn to be violent. This is the explanation of the spontaneous, muscular, sanguinary, and brutal character of Western man's violence; and of the willed, nervous, mental, hysterical character of Chinese violence.[6]

Moravia announces somewhat gratuitously: "The difference between Sartre, Camus and myself is that when I wrote *Gli Indifferenti* I was unaware that there was such a word as Existentialism," [7] but he calls, in a personal interview, for "a New Novel" whose precondition shall be "a new philosophical image of Man." What seems to be a contradiction is continued when he insists that the dilemma of his characters comes from his own imagination, and yet it is the concentration and extermination camps that provide "the most exact, consistent image of the modern world." [8] As an Italian author, then, Moravia, in the words of Buber, knows where he comes from and he feels deeply his continuity with Dante, Boccaccio, Machiavelli, Ariosto, Manzoni, Goldoni, while also claiming descendence directly from Dostoyevsky and Joyce and further back to Shakespeare, Cervantes, Rabelais ("I would give all to have written a book like *Gargantua*").[9] It can be said that Manzoni is his Hesiod and Boccaccio his Homer.

It is worthwhile to take a brief look at the development of the novel in Italy, keeping in mind that a fuller, more comprehensive study is available in Sergio Pacifici's book, *The Modern Italian Novel*. Though Italian story-telling has enjoyed a rich tradition of heroic romances, poetry, and novellas, the novel as a completely realized form was late in developing. Pacifici, in his study, points out that certain creative manifestations can only be realized in countries that have historically reached an appropriate degree of social, political, and cultural development and freedom. He argues, "If the novel did not emerge in Italy until the early part of the nineteenth century—almost a century later than in England and France—we must assume that the social, political, and cultural conditions were simply unfavorable, or unreceptive, to the new genre." [10]

Several factors had to evolve before Italy could develop a truly national literature. Not the least of these obstacles was the language itself. Until almost the middle of the nineteenth century, Latin was the esteemed literary language, and serious writers dared not use Italian or the vulgate, if they desired their work to be praiseworthy. Even though Dante had written his *Divine Comedy* in Italian, the poets and writers who came after him were convinced that their works would survive only in Latin. Thus, the use of Latin was rigidly adhered to. The novel's *raison d'être* is mass appeal; it must, therefore, speak to the masses in a national language which they can understand. Italy's development of the novel was not only thwarted by the lack of a national language, but illiteracy, too, presented a major stumbling block. For the novel's success is dependent upon a large literate audience.

Along with the problems of linguistic unity and illiteracy, Italy's persistent political upheaval interfered with the establishment of a national literature. For centuries Italy was politically fragmented into separate states ruled by despotic, treacherous men. As these states grew suspicious and jealous of each other, they often made alliances with foreign powers. These non-Italian powers, notably France, Spain, and Austria, exploited the disunity of Italy and managed to dominate her internal and foreign affairs until the beginning of the nineteenth century. Italy was not successful in ousting her foreign influences and establishing a national unity until as late as 1861.

It was Manzoni who made the first great breakthrough and established the novel as an accepted literary genre. Indeed, Manzoni must be considered the first modern Italian novelist. Not only was his use of Italian new and daring, but he used a new way of stylistic expression. His masterpiece, *The Betrothed* (published in 1827, with a final version in 1842) stood as the stylistic pattern for the novel for many years.

The early Italian novels, as exemplified by Manzoni, Federico de Roberto, Giovanni Verga, and Antonio Fogazzaro, deal with romantic love, patriotism, regional life and customs. After unification this interest dissipates, and the logical turning is inward. The evolution of the psychological novel begins. The earliest, and by far the greatest innovator in this area was Italo Svevo. He began writing novels at the end of the nineteenth century, and his work culminated in the extraordinary *Confessions of Zeno* in 1923. Svevo's stream-of-consciousness technique, irony and veiled humor, anti-heroes, and his dependence on psychoanalytical findings give his work a unique contemporary validity. Svevo must be considered Moravia's most direct literary ancestor.

Though Italy's development of the novel was considerably slower than that of other European countries, in the hands of such skilled artists as Svevo, Pirandello, Dino Buzzati, Federigo Tozzi, and finally Alberto Moravia, she has evidenced an astonishing literary maturity. Not only has Italy caught up, but her writers have attained worldwide respect and admiration as well.

The infrastructure of Moravia's career seems to depend on that literary existential psychoanalysis which Sartre has brandished with such aplomb in the cases of Baudelaire and Genet. Perhaps, in his discretion, Moravia anticipates the experiment when he autobiographically speaks of the conservatism of childhood and his habit each day of telling stories out loud to himself in some lonely place, adventure stories consisting of episodes that last an hour or so, to be picked up the next day at the exact point of interruption. This would seem to be a perfect rehearsal (before he could read or write) of his daily writing habits as a mature artist. How convenient it would be to see the author in the invalid who at nine is stricken by tuberculosis of the bone and who for nearly ten years must lead a life of incapacity, his potential activity converted into a rich fantasy life. But that would be nineteenth-century mythology posing as psychology. No, before he was nine, before he was stricken, the solitary boy by the summer sea was a proper bard launched on his life project. Once again, art and sickness are contingencies that give style to each other, but, perhaps, without perceptible cause or effect.

His first book, written when he was eighteen and published by the young man himself, had one of the greatest successes in modern Italian literature. He remained a prodigy until his exile in the mountains marked the end of one period and the start of another. However, in that first sensational novel, *Gli Indifferenti* (*The Time of Indifference*), the themes of a lifetime of literature are announced. The bourgeoisie, the indifferent ones, their rotted hopes and poses, the exposure of the absurd conscience—all this coming before the scandal of the "good people" and the full Fascist scenario. A born moralist!

Predictably, the literary psychologist of Rome objects to such a title, but to no avail. In his darkest moments, in his most terrible stories, there is always at least the implied, the elliptical option. Where Camus and Sartre keep their moral reactions in the fore of their imagery, Moravia, like Faulkner, lets himself be pushed by revulsion. This is counterphobia: crime and perversion— nihilism—must be searched out from under the appearances and the "filthy logic" of the man in the palace or the man in the street; the darkest closet must be flung open, and what is done after discovery is irrelevant in art.

Moravia is never moralistic but, like Gide, works in the very midst of morals, which, in the new lexicon, would be called an existential value system. These values are naturally translated into behavior. This is, of course, the reverse of life where behavior is abstracted normatively into right and wrong conduct (morals) and verbalized as sacred traditions (ethics). So, for the author to deny that he is a moralist implies that he is a moral relativist (never amoral; that would be a solecism for the novelist of behavior) in the popular and foolish sense of existentialism, or nihilism. But he himself provides the explanation—"treat every man as an end in himself." This humble recension of Kant is, of course, the assumed categorical imperative without which existentialism would lack all credibility.

So, to continue an image we will use again later, the existential author is like a good doctor who sees in the symptoms of disease the signs of life comingled with suffering, and whose reason for being is to heal. He works, beyond revulsion, in the familiarity of decay and the horror of the flesh, in the midst of the visceral antithesis, protected from infection only by his cunning and his unstated motive. The analogy to healing goes to the heart of existentialism. The root of the word "heal" is the same as the root of "hole," "whole," the same as "holy." Then if alienation (the separation of body, soul, thought, intrapsychically, and the separation of beings interpersonally) is illness, the reconciliation of flesh to spirit and flesh to flesh is the clue to healing, the holy wholeness.

To make a philosophical model: the nervous system in congruence with the value system in interaction with a Thou when both are bound to be free. This "holiness" of individuals in their reactions to the death-shock of nothingness is the "prophets and the laws" for the new philosophy. In summary, morals are irrelevant, much better replaced by manners and the social contract where holiness is all. Kazantzakis, Unamuno, Camus, Sartre, Buber, Moravia are all holy writers, secular witnesses, absurd fathers of the existential church.

Moravia is closer to Camus and the variety of existentialism that takes nature as its categorical imperative. The Greco-African view is less occidental than the rest. If for Sartre all relationships owe their maintenance to strife, then for the Algerian and the Italian there is both a grimmer and a more hopeful exegesis: there are no relationships, strife-bound or otherwise, only the potential for relationships. But this potential can be released— Camus reflects, "grief had saved us at the last moment." Or again, in Moravia, the therapy may be illness or infidelity or imprisonment; all varieties of non-Being are susceptible to intersection by a natural force like human need (sadism's undoing) or some natural intransigent— a tree, for instance, in one of his best-known tales.

For Moravia, as for the lyrical philosophers, the choice not to commit suicide is fraught with implication. He, too, has heard Nietzsche's enjoinder inside him—to say yea to anyone or anything is to say yea to all. Thus, sexuality without sadism may be I and Being as surely as it will have been It and non-Being with sadism.

All this brings us as close as we shall come to Moravia's secret and his first claim to irreplaceability. He goes beyond the eighteenth and nineteenth centuries' vision of love. Psychological love, the last century's recension of faith, is the alternative to a neurosis or, in our terms, to non-Being. Each banal Oedipus or quotidian Electra reaps his harvest of hysterical misery, each will sing his song on the golden psychoanalytic couch, and the cure will be, at best, an irony like Goethe's, "What business of yours is it if I love you?" Moravia shares Camus's innovation on this profane theme.

These two classicists of the Midi inevitably pick up the narrative in the short-story form so admirably suited to the secret moralist. For instance, in Camus's "Adulterous Woman" we find a heroine—one that might have been created by Moravia—sick at heart over the scandal of a wasted life. She had identified with her husband's fears and greeds, and he with hers. This identification, so obligatory in the modern short story, must be seen as an avatar of cannibalism—each makes the other disappear, consumes the other's Being. The adulterous woman has an ecstatic experience on the balcony of their room on a cold, brilliant, starred night. Something begins in the legs and rises up like sap through her being until she lies on her back filled with the falling stars. She is nauseated, she is orgasmic, she weeps; she has turned a corner in her life. Camus spells out superbly the desideratum or dream of the more quietly drawn Moravian protagonist whose body, in sensuous pantomime, asks, "How shall I be saved?"

The answer lies in the therapy of the "limit situation." So drenched in history and politics are we that the idea of this boundary situation almost always connotes a convulsive social confrontation. It is one of Moravia's most valuable contributions to have given us the private, intimate moment at the interface of a life, and then to draw an ellipsis over the scene in order to deny the gratification of our banal hankering for closure and symmetry. Moravia is concerned with those sore-spirited individuals whose vegetative irritability condemns them to collide with values they cannot tolerate; they must suffer in a game whose rules they cannot stomach, then, in the end, commit philosophical cannibalism and non-Being or, hopefully, find the game irrelevant and through acceptance of their finitude, become what they are. It is the moment of this becoming that all dramatic literature turns on; and by confining the area for this unspeakable struggle to the autosphere of the body in solitude, Moravia sets himself literature's most godlike task. This private limit situation is predominately inspired by one cause: the relationship between two potential lovers. To avoid this potential is to avoid the arena and the chance of authenticity. Moravia has thundered that those who attempt to avoid the big wars of love "are swine." [11] To derelict the commotions and convulsions of a love relationship is to be damned.

This, then, is the new logic: biology in collision with culture leads to repression or non-Being. Non-Being leads to angst and the attempt to rob the Other of his Being. Since this is true of the Other as well, a mutually cannibalistic bargain in panic and bad faith is made. For the dramatic character, bad faith leads to an extreme moment of radical choice when he must choose or suffer. Finally, with luck, the body takes over; the reason is cancelled; through fear and trembling the sap of Being and freedom rises shatteringly. This is the slow, then swift predicate for the luminous moment: the I-Thou. For, to paraphrase Malraux, quick reality comes only through bodies.

In the vicissitudes of love, the I-It and the I-Thou is a transition from matter—through matter, to spirit—to a love as different as the previous age's Romance was from the millennia of faith before it. This moment is evanescent, cannot be summoned or held; but the memory of it gives us something to go on. To stand open in the night of truth, like Moravia's or Camus's woman, in one's own bed or on a balcony, just once. The sap of life rises—whether it be nausea or ecstasy is irrelevant—and one is prepared for perhaps the first mature I-Thou experience.

The limit situation is the precursor to the I-Thou. The I-Thou can happen between strangers as well as intimates. Moravia, like Buber, seems to feel that members of the opposite sex are likely candidates for an attempt at a total relationship only because those of the same sex may be inherently more competitive.

What has happened, happens. This is the strange circular thinking of Buber as it was of Nietzsche and Kazantzakis. The eternal return based on choice. By this token it is sufficient for a Moravian character to love once, for has not our father, Dostoyevsky, taught us that "one day is enough" and that "hell is the state of being without love"? This existential love, standing on the corpse of nihilism, will come and go, no respecter of persons.

The I-Thou feeling is less radical than the one that comes from the extreme encounter. Less radical and, in stronger contrast, joyful. Moravia, with nature as his counter, shows us this occasional joy; a serious joy not euphoric, but rather a eudaemonism based on the inner capitulation to finitude and the final security in the knowledge that this painful finitude is coeval and coterminous with Being. Thus Moravia's characters adventure into relationships and into the world looking not for another person but for a showdown, an extreme situation that will open the channel for the vital current between mind-body-soul or kill them physically since they are already dead philosophically. Then, changed, they too will be candidates for the evanescent signals of selfhood. Now and then with the stranger (the stranger in themselves, in their lover, in the world) they will have that experience (less than catharsis, much less than ecstasy) that rewards the periods of trying and waiting in between.

Moravia as a skilled, sometimes caustic therapist brings his sufferers to their appointed moments of genetic or historical crisis (to take the two extremes); then we are permitted a glimpse at the patient in the epicrisis as reason returns; we are spared the convalescence and must only guess at the *Vita Nuova* ahead. At the moment of absurd hope the therapist draws the curtains between the patient and the visitor. Secrecy gives way to privacy.

This cure cannot come without the maintenance of good faith, after the lesson of the limit situation, so sensitive is our ruined conscience in this mournful age. This does not mean a clean white slate in the old sense, but rather one black with deeds and failures attempted in good faith and, always, with the value system and the nervous system in a congruence. The logic and imperatives of the flesh lead the way under the rule of finitude. It is the sense of finitude, provoked endlessly by Moravia, that leads to authenticity; for it keeps us from crimes against the Being of others because we know they are alone and without God too, and so no crime is permitted against them. Out of finitude we are finally compelled to heed Freud's ultimate injunction, "Give death its place." If existentialism can help us to do that it will lead us away from murder toward a new love.

There is one final and univocally existential common denominator for Alberto Moravia: mythomania. He shares with Sartre, Buber, Camus, and Unamuno the idea of man as actor—Nietzsche's dancer in a latter-day role. Man as actor, not as clock as in the eighteenth century, or man as machine in the nineteenth and twentieth centuries; these are now a vacated iconography.

After man eats his bread, everything else he may do is an act or role. He has no "character"; he plays roles. But, Sartre would add, therefore he is free! Free to play a role in good faith. For Camus the actor is *the* absurd man. For Unamuno the world is a stage, life a deliberate fiction, and man, if he chooses to be the actor, is authentic. He must play his role sincerely, for there is no evil without intent. Action and style alone redeem us from what the other "makes of us." We must not act out the fantasies of others. In the work of Moravia, one cannot help but notice the identity struggle of his creations' restless role-playing. His most memorable characters are defined by their hidden agendas and scenarios which finally open up under the pressures of finitude. This is an old existential dodge—the mad Nietzsche when he was called by name replied, "Me? No, I'm a fool."

Mythomania (it is Malraux's term) is the singular touch of the times, personally and collectively. When it is conscious, it is style and faith; when it is passively received, it is twitching and madness.

Let us be extremely clear. For Moravia and the existential artists, man is not a bundle of secrets; he is an actor of chosen roles.

Now that existentialism is approaching its third phase (first a new idea is preposterous, then it is obvious, then it is claimed by its enemies), we may wonder about its therapeutic destiny. Help for the soul is demanded in these days by the Western masses and any philosophy not relevant to the Via Veneto cannot last in a time of engaged stylists like Moravia.

The nineteenth-century men—the Dane, the Russian, the German, the men from countries where nobody lived—they would have been proud of their European sons in letters and in life. But now there are only two sons left. Buber, the older brother, is dead, and Kazantzakis, and also, unbearably, Albert Camus. Sartre and Moravia continue in the blood-red tradition of the saviors of God; they are in league with the great Combatant who, having escaped from plants and animals, now leaps inside our body demanding release into the overman. For we, to paraphrase Kanzantzakis, are the creatures that have been called Man too soon.

So as the century turns at bay, the man, Moravia, sits

each day at his orderly desk in his austere quarters, while outside, the "novel of fact," the Happening, all the postliterary media begin more and more to confront the man who now, more than any other, combines the psychological genius of the last age with the startling existential vision of the new day. With Sartre now lost to literature (thanks to the fury of the revolution of the Third World) the Italian's is, in a way, that "last voice" that Faulkner predicted would fill what some would call the last silence.

2

Man out of Love and Nature

Moravia's writing reveals his deep ties with nature; he loves the ocean, bright sunlight, rain, vegetation, and mountains. Over and over we find him extolling the wonders of the earth, giving nature prominence, using it as that symbol which brings man back to life, literally back to his senses.

It is evident that Moravia has learned much from his important predecessor, Italo Svevo. There are numerous parallels in the writing of the two Italians. Svevo is especially adept in using weather to relate a mood or feeling, although his use of nature is less common and somewhat more restrained than Moravia's. A passage from Svevo shows how much Moravia has absorbed from the earlier writer. In *As a Man Grows Older*, Emilio walks with his love to a hillside where they can observe the city at their feet.

> They remained folded in a long embrace, with the city at their feet, as silent and dead as the sea which, from that height, seemed one vast expanse of colour, mysterious, undefined. Motionless, there in the silence, city, sea and hills seemed to be all of one piece, if some artist had shaped and coloured all that matter according to his own strange fancy . . . The gradually increasing moonlight did nothing to change the

colour of the landscape . . . A snowy brilliance over-
spread it, motionless, while colour slumbered within
a shade of secret immobility even on the sea, whose
external movements one could just discern in the
silver play of water on its surface; colour was lost in
sleep. The green of the hills and all the many colours
of the houses were darkened, while the light which
saturated the outer air seemed to be suspended in
white incorruptible purity, inaccessibly removed from
contact with objects of our vision. The moonlight
seemed to have become incarnate in the girl's face so
near to his own . . . leaving . . . that golden glow
which it seemed to Emilio that he could actually
taste with his lips. Her face had become grave . . .
as he kissed it he felt himself to be more than ever a
seducer. He was kissing the pure virginal moonlight.[1]

This is masterly description, and Moravia, to his credit,
seems to have responded to a part of Svevo which re-
inforced his own sensibilities. Could it be that he absorbed something of Svevo which would later become
a major stylistic tool? Moravia exploits nature to a far
greater degree than Svevo, but with surely no more rich-
ness. Nature is eternal, mysterious, pure, and finally
sensuous in the existential pantheism.

In *The Empty Canvas*, Dino, in a frantic effort to end
his life, rams his car into a tree. This head-on collision
with reality holds many meanings. The tree, for Sartre,
is a symbol quite contrary to what it is for Moravia. To
the great Frenchman the tree in *Nausea* is pregnant and
sinister, bursting with danger. Moravia makes the tree
a life-saver in a strange way. Moravia, so much like
Camus in his reliance on the therapy of nature, makes
of the tree a life-shocking experience. Dino is almost
killed by this collision with nature, but his crisis and
convalescence lead to a far-reaching revival. For Moravia,

the interaction with nature and the fateful tree is crucial and full of pain, placing one's very life (physical, psychological, and philosophical) in jeopardy, and yet it cannot be avoided. This becomes, we will see, the showdown between nihilism and nature, love and death.

Often it is through nature that a character's disposition or the mood or "feeling" of a story is revealed. "The Chimpanzee," a story from *More Roman Tales*, begins significantly.

> Winter in Rome. I was going down the avenue in the Borghese Gardens . . . and all the time it was pouring with rain. But you could see each drop, as it came down, streaking the black sky with white, because the sun was shining brightly beyond the groves of trees, amongst luminous clouds that streamed away on every side. It was raining and the sun was shining; if I had not known it was January I should have thought it was March, so mild was the air, so tall and thick and green the grass in the plantations. It was raining in torrents . . . and the grass under the trees was drinking in both rain and sunshine alike. All at once I felt happy, and I felt a great strength in my legs as though I were a gigantic grasshopper, able to leap at one bound on the roof of the Museum . . . and I did actually leap into the air, opening my mouth towards the sky, and a drop of rain fell right into my mouth and seemed to intoxicate me as though I had taken a gulp of liquor.[2]

A coup! Here is Moravia's natural theme from another side. The grasshopperlike denial of gravity is clearly more than a euphoric mood-setting, more than an abrogation of a Newtonian law. Gravity, the grave, death itself and, most important, all that is earthbound is cancelled. But this dangerous delusion cannot last; it will have to be replaced by a hard-won, humble hope.

We follow the young mechanic as he meets his girl

for a date. He invites her to visit the zoo; she agrees to go, but not without protest. There, the day which started so beautifully, ends with a feeling of gloom. A chimpanzee hurls filth on the girl, she runs away screaming, and the young man is left alone. "I too went on my way, leaving the Zoo and going back up the avenue until I found myself again in the same place where, a couple of hours before, I had felt so happy. But now I felt crushed and depressed and the Borghese Gardens seemed the ordinary Borghese Gardens of every day and the same rain which had given me such pleasure before . . . now irritated me." [3] The day had become a dirty joke.

Again, in a story from *More Roman Tales*, Nature is used to convey a character's mood or feeling. "Pia was now sitting opposite me, in her mother's place. And I was looking at her and, seeing her in front of me in flesh and blood, I felt truly well, as one feels after spending a month in seaside sunshine and mountain air. Seaside sun and mountain air were, for me, Pia; and now she was actually in front of me and no longer did I have to go and seek the features of her face in the face of her mother." [4] As in the first story, Moravia repeats a persistent and urgent theme. Nature is seen as the giver of life; that force which sustains and nurtures life.

Interestingly, Svevo, too, sees nature as sustaining and life-giving. This exaltation is from *The Confessions of Zeno*.

The weather had become glorious again. The air was soft and delicious, and the countryside, still wet from the recent rain, was bathed in brilliant sunshine. After being confined to the office for so many days, my lungs expanded and I found it delightful to exercise my limbs. . . . Everything around me seemed to breathe out health and energy. Everywhere the young, green grass was springing; the catastrophic floods of a few days ago had sunk into the frozen earth, which now drank rapturously the sun-rays it had waited for so long. . . . At that moment my soul was filled with joy: joy in my own well-being and in the perennial well-being of nature.[5]

Moravia's concern with nature as life is so tenacious that he must often tell us the obvious. In "The Chimpanzee" he tells of the tall, thick, green grass drinking in both the rain and sun. The sheer sumptuousness of his description is bursting with growth and life. At other times this theme becomes a little more veiled, more symbolic. The young man in the second story who does not want to live without his beloved, compares her presence, her physical being with the therapeutic exposure to seaside sun and mountain air. Later, we shall carry these two persistent Moravian nature themes— fertility and sustenance—to their logical and final ramification in sexuality.

Sensitive descriptions of nature are put to brilliant use in two stories from *The Fetish*. In "The Strange Land," an aimless young man reflects: "It had rained for three days; and a woodland smell, evoked by the warm, abundant rain of autumn, rose up from the piles of dead leaves in the suburban avenue. This smell gave him a sudden desire for happiness, which for him, at that moment, would have meant being conscious of doing things that he liked." [6] In this story, Tolstoy-like, Lucio is bitterly aware that he sees people he ought not to see, goes where he doesn't want to go, and does things he isn't interested in. He recognizes the sterility and bareness of his life. After a meaningless visit to an extremely eccentric young woman whose absurd behavior leads them into a savage fight, Lucio leaves and the story conveys a mood using nature, as it did at the beginning.

In the wide suburban street, as he walked along beside the plane-trees, he noticed once again the woodland smell awakened by the autumnal rains and became aware that, by contrast, he was acutely and stupidly unhappy. Was it possible, he thought, that his life could never resemble that smell, so good and so alive; and that he was condemned, on the other hand, to do things and to be with the people he did not like? [7]

Lucio's stupid, absurd existence is again brought home to him as he contemplates the "purity" of nature. Juxtaposing it against nature, "so good and so alive," Moravia makes an especially effective study of Lucio's feeling of absurdity. Unlike "The Chimpanzee," where the mood was first happy, then depressed, this story reflects the reverse. The closing lines denote a turn for the better, an affirmation of change. "He realized that he found no enjoyment in anything and did not understand anything; like a stranger in a strange land who is forced, before he can find his bearings, to make a number of mistakes. But this comparison, which before had appeared to him disheartening, now comforted him a little. After the mistakes, who knows? he went on to think, perhaps the right things would emerge." [8]

In a second story from *The Fetish*, "The Automaton," Guido registers the world.

His eyes, meanwhile, took note of a quantity of things which seemed interesting but whose significance escaped him—the glitter on the chromium plating of a big black car in front of them, the immaculate whiteness, speckled with points of light, of a cylindrical petrol-tank half hidden amongst the budding trees of spring . . . a sudden flash from a window struck by a ray of sunshine, the chalky tinge of the warning lines painted on the trunks of the plane-trees along the road. All these white, gleaming, flashing things contrasted stridently with a big black cloud which had spread over the sky and threatened to spoil the fine day; the landscape, too, of a bright, tender, almost milky green, was out of harmony against the dark, stormy background. Once again Guido wondered what could be the significance of this contrast, but he could find no solution: and yet he was sure there was one.[9]

This near-hypnotic reverie, as he drives his wife and children on an outing, contains an ominous note that echoes a banal but disturbing incident that has occurred at their new flat before leaving. The American record player, an automatic, had perversely gone wrong, scratching and ruining a disc of light music. Guido, who is already hypercritical of his stylish new clothes, is unable to overcome this mechanical breakdown. Added to these disturbances is the nagging feeling of having forgotten something. Thus plagued, he drives the family along on their Sunday outing and like a camera records the milky, green landscape and the dark, stormy background.

Suddenly Guido felt as if he were coming out of a long tunnel into the open, emerging from a close, stagnant atmosphere into the clear, light air . . . there came to him a precise thought—to drive the car at full speed into the void beyond the top of the hill, to hurl himself, together with his wife and children, into the lake.[10]

At the last moment he is distracted by an unexpected meadow. Shaken, he pulls over, they get out to view and he remembers what had eluded him so maddeningly all day—his wedding anniversary, around which the whole trip had been planned.

Here is a very short story ripe with nature imagery both dark and light, hopeful and fearful, and the will toward nothingness: Moravia at his most economical and over-determined. The broken gramaphone, the machine?

The broken machine, the broken cortex. This is a central twentieth-century symbol, one that surpasses the dead God in literary influence. For us God has been dead now almost a hundred years; we are well adjusted to that liberating fact. In the driver's seat is the machine and its double, the cortex. But what, ask the artists, if we have bargained and lost, exchanged the old God for a power we are unable to collect? Of course, this is precisely what has happened. It is not that machines may go wrong. We stand here at *anus mundi* in the shadow of the apogee of ratiocination (the machine): the Camps and the Bomb. The realpolitik political machine and the physical; the weaponry revolution and a world starving to death; these dark images rise before us while over against them, in Camus's "unequal struggle," is the new litany, "make love not war, world without end": those radical and aesthetic coalitions that have begun to interdict the wheels and the gears, the levers and the pulleys of the machine of the Establishment. So, God is dead; but secular, vain man is unable to bear the news that the machine is dead as well. If we are not His children any more neither are we Its servomechanism either. The world's worst-kept secret is out: we are free and the swindle is concluded. These still-rough feelings are a part of a new criticism as surely as they are one of the contexts for the important writing of this century.

The failed arm and needle of the record machine in "The Automaton" are, at the same time, a physico-psychological as well as a metaphysical metaphor. *Impotenza*, the old Italian tune, is there, the identification of the I with the It, and the angst of this merger. Then, on toward the limit situation, with the image, mobile and challenging, of the emergence "from the close, stagnant atmosphere into the clear, light air." Another conversion point; this time it is a passage through evocative, "thick, furry green slopes." And beyond the belvedere a sheer drop; simple nothingness, nihilism and nostalgia call; the boundary situation Guido struggles to remember. He looks into the abyss, and "it seemed to him that he had never loved them [his family] so much as at this moment when he desired to destroy them"[11] (he confuses the coeval nostalgia for nothingness and the rising love of his family); he remembers! He is not an automaton; Guido remembers the anniversary of his marriage (his love). This is the very rhythm and sign of the I-Thou!

In a variation on the obsession with nature, it is interesting to note that in describing his characters, Moravia often makes comparisons to animals. This seems to be one more subtle way he communicates man's "instinctual" (natural) or "animal" character. It is as if by aligning certain facial characteristics or gestures with those of animals, the reader is caught in the suspicion or awareness of man's compromised "nature." The comparison is not always meant to be unflattering or to convey ferocity; many times the description is a charming one. In a story from *More Roman Tales*, Massimina is pictured as "a short, broad young woman, with a small, round head whose retreating curves and curly hair make it look like the head of a small sheep . . . she had become broad all over, though still retaining, for me at any rate, the characteristic charm of a little curly-headed sheep."[12]

In a story from *The Fetish* a pretty young woman is described, "Signora Cecilia was very like some kind of exotic bird with a tiny body and an enormous, fantastic head."[13] Also from *The Fetish*, "As he came close to her, he saw that she was very young and not without a certain rustic beauty of her own. Her face round, with a noble, authoritative expression, her hair thick and puffed out; she had rather piercing eyes, a small aquiline nose

which looked like the beak of a bird of prey, and a big,
arrogant mouth." [14] A provocative description is found
in *The Lie*.

> It was still the same face, rather like that of a pirate
> in a book of adventure stories for boys; but the long
> face, the drooping mustache, the hooked nose, the
> thick eyebrows, which ten years ago had gone to make
> up a living physiognomy, even if of rather a conven-
> tional kind, now had the frivolous, empty, artificial
> look of a mask. I noticed this particularly from the
> eyes. Consolo's eyes had been like those of a faithful
> dog—moist, cheerful, ingenuous, a little crazy. Now,
> beneath the two frowning thickets of his eyebrows,
> they appeared fixed and glassy, like those of a stuffed
> animal. [15]

Moravia seems to use his impressive animal imagery
in two ways. First, he picks up a traditional and now
existential idea: after a certain age people are responsible
for their persona, their looks and their style. Looks equal
character equal choices (choices first forced on one and
then chosen). The second employment is more original.
It would seem that the *resemblance* among all animals,
rather than their dissimilarities, strikes Moravia. He sees
a unity, a solidarity, where we want to see a viciously
anthropocentric world. This aristocratic, thoroughly civ-
ilized author is, in his deepest vision, primitive and pan-
theistic, both loyal to and critical of all life.

An examination of *Bitter Honeymoon* shows further
instances of primitive, instinctual nature revealed
through allusions to animallike characteristics. "At the
time of his arrival all the rooms except the one next to
Sandro's were untenanted; and the first time he went
out on to the wide balcony he immediately saw the oc-
cupant of that one. It was a young and beautiful girl
with magnificent fair hair and a face that bore a close

resemblance to a little pig." [16] In the same story another woman is described. "The slightness of her forehead and her huge eyes made one think of some animal. And her sharp, chiselled nose, her thin cheeks that seemed to find their outlet in her wide, full mouth, confirmed this impression of animality. It was a face that suggested to one's mind the muzzle of a goat, a tame goat, mad and a trifle obscene." [17] In a second story from *Bitter Honeymoon* a young husband observes his wife. "Over her sunburnt face and red mouth her freckles and the soft down on her lip threw a veil of shadowy sensuality. But her eyes, small and black, gazed obstinately ahead, and the upward sweep of her hair from her forehead gave her whole appearance an aggressive, hard look. She had something simian about her, Lorenzo thought; manifest not so much in her features as in her sad, decrepit and innocent expression, like that of some small monkeys. And like a monkey she put up a pretense of offended dignity which he knew she was quite incapable of." [18]

Perceiving the animal in man seems to be a function of the twentieth-century demystification of the human being. If God is dead then man must give up his vicarious megalomania; he is only an animal. But here a secret solace begins: if he is an animal then he must exist only in the present like a newspaper or a wild beast, and from day to day to day he will know the despair and the exhilaration, the cruelty of choice. This cruelty is the price of his manhood. "Animal" begins to lose its pejorative ring. Man is not lower than the angels because there are no angels, and by the same token his world view is at ground level, horizontal. The hierarchy is broken; the human's gaze levels off, he looks around him, the glance is at eye level, bruised and wiser. But he is different from the other animals. But of course—we are the animals who bind time. We remember at many levels of abstraction. History, nostalgia—it is all the same yearning.

Of a Gestapo agent, in *Days of Wrath*, Malraux has the prisoner Kassner think:

> he resembled both a walrus Kassner had seen in Shanghai and the fat Chinese who was displaying him. Kassner knew his own mania for finding a resemblance to an animal in every face.

Not just the Gestapo but all men are animals. This perception is beyond good and evil; it is sheer existential irony. Men, as Gorky said, are like beetles. They're all black and they're all good jumpers.

In *Luca*, Moravia tells of an adolescent's complete alienation and physical collapse. The descriptions of Luca's breakdown are numerous and minutely detailed. One of these descriptions is pertinent to this discussion. "Sometimes his body seemed to give way beneath him, as an exhausted horse, dull-eyed with fatigue, gives way beneath the rider who vainly spurs it on." [19] This story is enhanced by some of Moravia's most beautiful nature-mood passages.

> After a few fine days winter had resumed its course and it rained most of the time. The rain descending from a pitch-black sky seemed to be dark and opaque, as though it were mixed with mud, and it spread everywhere a darkness which made Luca feel it would be pleasant to curl up and go to sleep for good. Sometimes, as he did his lessons, he would raise his eyes toward the window and feel convinced that the sky was clearing. He would become absorbed in his work; half an hour later he would look up again and be astonished at the sight of the heavy, gray rain flowing in silent waves down the windowpanes. The sky was like a person weeping in some profound sorrow, who seems every now and then to grow calmer and more serene but who is soon caught up again by grief and

starts once more to shed tears, more abundantly and more violently than ever." [20]

Luca's I-It, I-Thou fluctuations between inertia and work, sickness and health are beautifully symbolized here by the black sky which at one time clears only to weep with rain in another instance. Several pages later the author uses the same means to pursue Luca's state of limbo.

The weather was bad but still undecided, with a low, dark sky which had not yet resolved to shed the rain which burdened it. Occasionally a gust of damp wind stirred the mild, motionless air; then Luca would see all the leaves of the trees in the gardens turn over with a flash of silver, while coils of gray dust rose hissing at the street corners from the dry stones of the pavements. But the wind would fall again at once, and the paving stones remained dry. It was a kind of weather that resembled his own state of mind, and it seemed to him they were like each other in the way they both waited for something to happen. In the end, possibly, it would rain; in the end, possibly, he would come to a decision. [21]

This important work will be discussed in depth in a later section. Sufficient here, is the recognition of the stunning way in which nature is used to herald Luca's indecision and futility and eventual surrender to his inner grief, the rain symbolizing the tears that well up more "abundantly and violently than ever."

The use of nature stems not only from a deep love and attachment, but also from a feeling of the capacity of nature to make man complete. Furthermore, we do violence to man in overlooking what is most elemental, most instinctual, most primitive in him. Moravia is aware of the important and essential role of instinct in retaining and explaining man's humanness. Instinctual nature cannot be violated without violating life itself. It must be recalled the way love recalls Guido (though he thinks he remembers his anniversary). The return, the eternal return is signalled when the machine breaks; finitude pours into the automaton, almost killing him (like Faulkner's boy who, hopelessly lost in familiar woods, threw away his compass at the moment of crisis). We are lost in familiar woods. The acceptance of finitude makes the landscape recognizable again. God has been killed not so that man can fill the category but so that he can be Man.

The significance of nature for Moravia is overall. The preceding section has tried to make clear the extent of this powerful influence. Indeed, Moravia emerges as absolutely dependent upon nature. This therapeutic dependence is utilized brilliantly to create moods, describe emotions, or shape a character's persona. Recognition of the anaclitic relationship of the author to nature is essential if we are to progress to a more complete understanding of Moravian reality.

3

Alienation

Moravia's characters, from the young brother and sister in his first novel to the antihero in one of his latest novels, suffer the pangs of terrible alienation. An inability to relate themselves to reality leaves his men and women hollow and empty, struggling with an existence which often reveals itself as shameful, false, and pretentious.

How does this modern malady of alienation disclose itself in Moravia's people? Do his characters really suffer at all? If so, how does he indicate this particular kind of suffering? And, further, how is this pointless suffering through alienation resolved into meaningful suffering? A close scrutiny of the works themselves will provide answers to these questions.

And, we should inquire, is this alienation from God, from nature, or from the self? Alienation from nature would mean alienation from the self and from the love of the I-Thou, for nature and the I are but recensions of each other, with love as a focused derivative inside the flesh. Moravia deals primarily with this estrangement from the two extremes of the world and the I. For him, the alienation is not historical nor psychological. He is not shooting his way out of alienation and into history like the third world revolutionary (which he understands as completely as if he were a white translator for Fanon, and he is, perhaps, Sartre's only equal in this sphere), nor talking his way out of an unconscious bundle of secrets into time and the ego like the shivering analysand on his couch of therapy and suffering.

In *The Time of Indifference*, his first novel written at the age of nineteen, we are confronted with a picture of alienation at once shocking and oppressive. Written at the end of the author's long convalescence from tuberculosis, the work projects an inner vision of estrangement, frightening in its sickness and malignancy. *Time of Indifference* is a ferocious indictment of the falseness which infects contemporary society. The youthful Moravia lays bare the corruption, baseness, and sham which characterize modern man's preoccupation with material wealth and prosperity.

Moravia's young protagonists, a brother and sister, see through the hypocrisy of the adults around them. In a discussion with Leo, her mother's lover, Carla pours forth a flood of hatred against her stupid, bickering mother. "If you only knew . . . how oppressive, how miserable, how shabby all this is, and what kind of life one leads, having to listen to it all every day, every single day." [1] Leo challenges her to break away and she declares that in the end this is what she will do, but "she felt she was acting a part that was both false and ridiculous." [2] Overcome with lust, Leo attempts to persuade the confused girl to come away with him.

> Again she made the futile gesture of trying to push him away from her, but more feebly than before, for now a kind of resignation had taken possession of her: why should she refuse Leo? Virture would merely throw her back into the arms of boredom and the distasteful trivialities of everyday habit; and it seemed to her, furthermore, . . . that this present adventure, with its air of familiarity, was the only epilogue her

old life deserved; afterwards, everything would be new—both life and herself. . . . End it all, she thought, ruin everything. And her brain whirled as though she were about to hurl herself head foremost into space.[3]

Again, later, we read Carla's thoughts as she reveals herself caught in a hopeless and pathetic struggle against indifference and futility.

She noticed then, for the first time, how stale, how ordinary, how distressing was the scene in front of her —her mother and her mother's lover sitting opposite each other in a conversational attitude; the half-darkness, the lamp, the blank, stupid faces, and she herself leaning affably on the back of the armchair to listen and talk. Life doesn't change, she thought, it refuses to change. She wanted to scream; she lowered her hands and wrung them together, against her belly, so violently that her wrists ached. . . . There was nothing to be done, for everything was immutable, everything was ruled by a king of shabby fatality.[4]

Caught in this web of shabby fatality, Carla consents to become Leo's mistress. Though she hopes that this will be a significant step toward changing her life, it is, in reality, no more than a repetition of the falseness which she has always known. Alone in her own room, Carla seems to sense the falseness of her decision.

"A new life really *is* beginning," she said to herself. . . . and suddenly it seemed to her that this quiet, innocent, unsuspecting room, these familiar things, partly shabby and partly silly, made up, altogether, a living entity, a single person with a clearly defined figure, for whom she was in the process of preparing, secretly and without any fuss, a monstrous betrayal. . . . "Isn't it strange? . . . tomorrow I am going to

give myself to Leo and thus a new life should begin
. . . and it so happens that tomorrow is the day on
which I was born." She remembered her mother. And
it is with *your* man, she thought, with *your* man,
Mom, that I'm going. Even this ignoble coincidence,
this rivalry with her mother, pleased her; everything
must be impure, dirty, low, there must be neither love
nor affection, but only a dark sense of ruin. "I must
create a scandalous, impossible situation, full of
scenes and hopelessly shameful . . . I must ruin myself utterly." . . . it seemed to her that these melancholy thoughts had already destroyed her. "Where is
my life going?" She kept asking herself. . . . These
grievous words, in the end, held no more meaning for
her; and she realized that she was no longer thinking
. . . and of the exaltation of a few minutes earlier
there remained nothing but empty bitterness.[5]

"Tomorrow is the day on which I was born." This is
pure existentialism in the diction of an adolescent.
Moravia gives us an agonizing picture of the alienation
which plagues Carla's younger brother. Michele would
like to be looked up to. He would like to rival Leo as a
figure of strength and force on whom his mother can
lean, for Mariagrazia, the mother, once a wealthy woman,
now faces burdensome mortgage payments. The unscrupulous Leo magnanimously offers to buy the family
villa—at much less than the true value. Michele yearns
to expose the villainous Leo, but over and over again he
gives way to feelings of complete indifference.

No action on Leo's part, however villainous, was
capable of shaking his indifference; after a sham out-
burst of hatred, he always ended by finding himself as
he was now, somewhat dazed and lightheaded, his
mind empty. . . . the image of himself as he really
was and as he could not forget that he was, pursued

him. He seemed to have a clear vision of himself—
alone, wretched, indifferent. . . . But his anguish
was increasing. . . . he already knew the course it
would take: first the vague uncertainty, the lack of
confidence, the sense of emptiness, the need to busy
himself with something, to find some passionate interest; then, very gradually, the dry feeling in the
throat, the bitter taste in the mouth . . . the insist-
ent recurrence of certain absurd phrases in his vacant
mind, a state, in fact, of furious and disillusioned despair. Of this state of anguish Michele had a most
painful dread: he longed not to think about it, but to
live, like everybody else, from minute to minute, with
no anxieties, at peace with himself and with others.
. . . Once upon a time, it appeared, men used to
know their paths in life from the first to the last step;
but now it was not so; now one's head was in a bag,
one was in the dark, one was blind. And yet one still
had to go somewhere; but where? [6]

In a bag! Moravia's very phrase strikes a note so true
that it is small wonder that the term "bag" has become
synonymous with alienation. This first novel creates the
very ambience and terms of existentialism: "but where?
where can I find my home?" cried Neitzche.

Overcome with despondency and futility, Michele
and Carla are powerless to act or rebel against an environment which holds them captive. Their alienation is
one against the ego (I)—an I which, aware and sensitive, has seen through the frantic clamor after money
and possessions but is incapable of acting. This is what
makes their outsidedness all the more acute and tragic.
Too weak to muster the stamina to fight a creeping alienation, they give themselves over to it with a vengeance.
They identify with the aggressor (nothingness). Their
philosophical suicide is an annihilation of the world, but
it is, of course, like every other gesture, manqué.

Moravia makes the confrontation with inauthenticity forceful and direct, but his characters are nevertheless overcome with *impotenza*. They can see, they understand, but the final test proves too much for them. A sickening neurotic mother and her unscrupulous lover have relentlessly forced Michele and Carla onto a path of outsidedness. Devoid of the autonomous conscience that would demand rejection of their false surroundings, they capitulate and are eventually trapped by their own indifference. This "indifference," like Chekov's "boredom," is, of course, not simply a feckless apathy (that is only a defense surface appearance), but a profound deracination; finitude (nothingness) rising like a tide through the viscera, the cortex rationalizing, repressing, projecting, denying, like a gyroscope wildly out of control and all the life force inverted in the unequal struggle, while on the surface a languid yawn is the only sign. But Moravia understands that this yawn is a world-cracking scream beyond the range of hearing, like a filmed cry for help with the sound turned off. He is, as always, the therapist who dares to hear the "dark root of the scream."

Carla and Michele bear a striking resemblance to many of Svevo's antiheroes. Svevo's characters are consistently overcome with futility and hopelessness. They are rarely fully engaged. Hesitant, entertaining misconceptions about themselves, they wander aimlessly about from one failure to another. However, in analyzing the characters delineated by these two writers, important differences are also revealed. A total view of Moravia shows that his men and women usually act affirmatively in a hostile world. But Svevo's bunglers are frequently defeated by reality. To Svevo life and reality are enemies which cannot be subdued and his characters are unable to master their own destinies.

Another superb example of alienation which manifests itself in meaningless suffering is found in *Luca*.

This short novel focuses on an adolescent's complete withdrawal from the world around him. Luca's withdrawal becomes so acute that it brings about a grave illness. His rejection leads him to reactions and feelings that are progressively more and more damaging. His environment fills him with rage, disgust, and then nausea, apathy, and indifference. Finally, he revolts through nihilism and a death wish.

> Another storm of rage came upon him in the train, shortly before he arrived home from his summer holiday. . . . The idea of lunch in a dining car had immediately delighted him, for he had never been in one. . . . Besides, Luca was extremely sensitive about the opinion of other people and about the formalities of decorous behavior. He had a wholehearted loathing of meals eaten on one's knees in a railway carriage, among dirty pieces of paper and fruit peelings and leftovers, with cold, greasy food squashed between the two halves of a gaping roll of bread. During such meals there was always somebody waiting to go to the dining car who would look on with an air of self-satisfaction and disgust at the family crouching over paper bags.[7]

As the journey progresses, Luca's parents once again decide to buy lunch baskets instead of going to the dining car.

> Luca nevertheless, though he realized that the decision had not been made out of spite, flew into a violent rage. What offended him most was that neither of them asked his opinion and that they treated him as an inanimate object, which, being a mere object, had neither preferences nor ideas, neither tastes nor wishes. . . . He went white in the face, clenched his teeth tightly and shut his eyes. He felt

himself grow stiff all over with the violent rage that tautened his body; for a moment he felt impelled to open the door and throw himself out of the train. This suicidal temptation did not frighten him, nor did it seem to him absurd; it was as he realized, the natural outlet of the furious feeling of impotence that overwhelmed him.[8]

Reluctantly, Luca does manage to eat some of the lunch his father buys.

And upon his stomach he felt the weight of the food he had eaten, like a big, tightly closed package done up in grease-proof paper, full of partly chewed bits and pieces, exactly like the paper bags full of odds and ends that housewives throw out of the windows into the alleys for the cats of the neighborhood.[9]

Luca is overcome by intense feelings of nausea. As the journey ends and they leave the train, he can no longer control this wave of sickness.

The engineer, his face smoke-stained and greasy, was looking at the people and devouring . . . what looked to Luca like a kind of green and yellow slush— a spinach omelette. At the sight of the omelette, he was conscious of an even more violent feeling of nausea, as though a current of sympathetic attraction like between a magnet and a piece of steel had come into being between the slush that the engineer was so eagerly devouring and that other slush that was fermenting in his own stomach. Now they had reached the buffers of the engine; he leaned on one of the headlamps and vomited against the great fuming machine. . . . it seemed to him that having vomited upon the engine had been, in a way, an act of revenge against the train which had brought him back so ruthlessly to the town, to school, to his lessons; in just the same way that his parents, ruthlessly, had refused him the dining car.[10]

In describing the lunches eaten on trains—"the family crouching over paper bags"—Moravia uses a diagnostic, bestial humor. We are filled with sympathy for Luca's suffering. Enraged over his parent's treatment of him as a "mere object," their insensitivity, and his own impotence to make his wishes known, Luca is forced to neurotic, meaningless behavior. At the end of the journey, his revenge must be spewed forth on the train.

Once home, Luca finds it more and more difficult to relate himself to school and his studies; like Guido, he detects in his mind an ominous presentiment which gradually expresses itself as a death wish. "He was aware of a bitter, unreasonable sadness, a sadness of resignation that made his acts wearisome and conscious, as though each act was an irrevocable step upon a fatal path." [11] Luca muses over "the utter bareness of his life"; [12] ordinary, automatic, habitual actions are exposed in all their absurdity.

And with this sense of the total absurdity of all that up till then had never been absurd, he recognized that the long course of his crisis was coming to an end. There was nothing more to be done but give a slight shake and the irksome membrane would drop away. He guessed that this shake, and nothing else, was the object of his presentiment.[13]

A complete physical collapse keeps Luca ill and in bed for three months, "he no longer wished to die; he was certain he *would* die and that certainty satisfied him." [14] But even as he gives himself over to death, he must still grapple with the powerful instinct to live.

Under these conditions, the duplicity which had entered into his life from the day when death had appeared to him as the only solution to the problem of his relations with the world—that duplicity now became intensified till it attained the kind of shrill coherence of a comedy of errors. With his parents he played, in a docile manner, the now entirely detached role of the invalid who is going to get well, of the scholar who is going to return to his studies, of the boy who is going to grow up and become a man; but, the moment he was alone, he became merely the dying man, fully conscious and contented, who watches for the approach of his end with a mind filled with hope.[15]

As Luca's illness progresses he is seized with terrifying hallucinations and delirium. Alarmed, his parents summon a nurse to care for him.

And then one day, sitting beside him, in the act of supporting his forehead with one hand and feeding him with the other, he saw a woman whom he did not know. . . . Her head was wrapped, it seemed to him, in a kind of white turban, beneath which her face looked brown and somewhat wasted but well-preserved. . . . This face was held erect, with a bird-like vanity, upon a long, rounded neck; and when he stammered out some confused words of thanks, the carefully made-up eyes, drowned in their paint and their wrinkles, held a spark of sympathy. . . . He made a movement as though to show that the light tired his eyes; and the woman at once rose and went to the window. She was all in white and Luca saw that small, well-preserved head of hers, like the head of some Oriental bird, was set upon a massive body.[16]

This kind nurse will watch over him, initiate him through sexual intercourse, recall him to life.

Then, as the fog of delirium gradually cleared away, although he was in a state of utter prostration following the fall of temperature, he noticed a strange thing which to him was entirely new. The nurse, in spite of being middle-aged and having lost her looks, the room which he had once hated, every single object, in fact, appeared to him in a new light—serene, clean, familiar, lovable, and so to speak, appetizing. . . . The nurse went away next day, as she had announced; and Luca was left with a feeling neither of regret nor of disgust, but rather of gratitude for his final initiation not merely into physical love but also into that more general love for all things, the first glimmer of which had reached him when he awoke from his delirium. He felt he had at last found a new and quite personal way of looking at reality—a way that was composed of sympathy and patient expectation. This way of looking at things, he observed, permitted a rhythm of thought much calmer, much fuller, much more serene than before, and with it a vision that was no longer direct and aggressive but scrupulously, ineffably hesitant and cautious. Now, he thought, he would see things first with those new eyes which had opened that night inside him, and only afterward with the eyes which at his birth had been dazzled by the first light of day. Second and truer mother, the nurse had given him a second birth when, in his desire for death, he had been already dead. But he knew that this second birth could never have taken place if he had not first desired, so sincerely, so wholeheartedly, to die.[17]

Luca's parents arrange for him to spend a period of convalescence at a sanitorium in the mountains. As the novelette ends, Moravia gives us one last exalted glimpse of Luca's conversion.

Luca closed his eyes. At that same moment the train, with a long and mournful whistle, plunged into a tunnel. When he opened his eyes again he saw nothing but darkness, while a damp wind blew in his face from the dark walls of the tunnel. . . . Echoing from the vault of the tunnel, the beat of the wheels sounded to him like a montonous, exultant voice repeating the same words over and over again. He seemed to be able to distinguish these words—the same words, full of hope, that had born him company ever since his awakening from delirium, day to day during his slow recovery; and he knew that, from now onward, not only the clatter of a train in a tunnel or the whiteness of snow on a mountain peak, but all things would have a meaning for him and would speak to him in their own mute language. Then the train, with another whistle, came out into the light of day.[18]

In a masterly stroke, Moravia has used the train, that very vehicle upon which Luca had earlier vented his rage and frustrations, as the object which finally transports him back to life. An overdetermined use of the same symbolism invested with new or different meaning; beginning and ending a story with the same nature-mood sequence; this always relevant circling back is a Moravian specialty handled with great artistry. The Nietzschean full circle, *amor fati*, and eternal rebirth and return.

The last paragraph reveals the tightly-knit sign of the entire story. The first "long and mournful whistle" signals Luca's illness and eventual break with reality; this plunging into the tunnel and experiencing "nothing but darkness" is certainly the death wish. In the beat of the wheels sounding first like a "monotonous, exultant voice," then like the repetitious words full of hope we feel the presence of the warmhearted nurse whose sympathy and words of encouragement, "you'll get well now," sustained him after the delirium. Finally, as now "all things would have a meaning for him and would speak to him in their own mute language," Luca's suffering has ended; he no longer feels alienation. With a last, exuberant shriek—"the train, with another whistle" —Luca, born again, rushes out "into the light of day" to embrace life, to be propelled into reality.

In a major work, *The Empty Canvas*, Moravia presents us with a slowly progressing and prolonged, minutely detailed study of estrangement through a hideous boredom. It is unfortunate that the Italian title *La Noia*, meaning "boredom," was not retained in the English translation. This is perhaps one of the most brilliant dissections of boredom in all contemporary literature. The most Sartrean of Moravia's novels, it is to Italian letters what *Nausea* is to modern French writing. The two works have many parallels; Dino and Roquentin are indeed soul mates. In symbolizing modern man's struggle for self-assertion and an authentic sense of existence, both artists have pictured the existential human being who wrestles with nothingness and death.

In *The Empty Canvas*, the hero, or in this case anti-hero, is a wealthy young man who decides to become a painter and desperately hopes "to be able to re-establish contact with reality, once and for all, by means of artistic expression." [19] Dino soon recognizes he has been wrong; his idea that painting would remedy his boredom is a delusion. He gives up painting and the canvas remains empty.

The story begins with Dino's admission that he has, as far as he can recall, always suffered from boredom. As a young boy, he conceived of a project for a universal history "according to boredom."

> My universal history according to boredom was based on a very simple idea: the mainspring of it was neither progress, nor biological evolution, nor economic development, not any of the other ideas usually brought forward by historians of various schools; it was simply

boredom. Burning with enthusiasm at this magnificent discovery, I went right to the root of the matter. In the beginning was boredom, commonly called chaos. God, bored with boredom, created the earth, the sky, the waters, the animals, the plants, Adam and Eve; and the latter, bored in their turn in paradise, ate the forbidden fruit. God became bored with them and drove them out of Eden; Cain, bored with Abel, killed him; Noah, bored to tears, invented wine; God, once more bored with mankind, destroyed the world by means of the Flood; but this in turn bored Him to such an extent that He brought back the fine weather again. And so on. The great empires—Egyptian, Babylonian, Persian, Greek and Roman—rose out of boredom and fell again in boredom. . . . All these fine discoveries were noted down by me in a kind of summary, then I began with great enthusiasm to write the true and proper history. . . . Then I grew bored with the whole project and abandoned it.[20]

There is a remarkable parallel to this code in a soliloquy of Sartre's Roquentin in *Nausea*.

We were a heap of living creatures, irritated, embarrassed at ourselves, we hadn't the slightest reason to be there, none of us; each one confused, vaguely alarmed, felt *de trop* in relation to others. *De trop*: it was the only relationship I could establish between these trees, these gates, these stones. In vain I tried to count the chestnut trees, to *locate* them by their relationship to the Velleda, to compare their height with the height of the plane trees: each of them escaped the relationship in which I flowed. . . . And I—soft, weak, obscene, digesting, juggling with dismal thoughts—I, too, was *de trop*. . . . Even my death would have been *de trop*. *De trop*, my corpse, my blood on these stones . . . and the decomposed flesh would have been *de trop* in the earth which received my bones, at last; cleaned, stripped, peeled, proper and clean as teeth, it would have been *de trop*: I was *de trop* for eternity.[21]

More clinical, greater despair—yet how revealing to watch Moravia and Sartre, in a long comparison, repeat to the point of silence or madness their euphemisms for what used to be called "a fall" and before that "damnation." Conscious, saving panic is replaced by boredom; one yawns and turns from the death-camp documentary.

Thus, in *The Empty Canvas* after deciding to give up painting, Dino proceeds to analyze exactly what boredom means to him. "Boredom to me consists in a kind of insufficiency, or inadequacy, or lack of reality. . . . The feeling of boredom originates for me in a sense of the absurdity of a reality which is insufficient, or anyhow unable, to convince me of its own existence." [22] As long as external objects can be related to himself in a convincing manner, Dino believes in the existence of these objects. When no relationship can be established, the object appears absurd—"Then from that very absurdity springs boredom, which when all is said and done is simply a kind of incommunicability and the incapacity to disengage oneself from it. . . . For me, therefore, boredom is not only the inability to escape from myself but is also the consciousness that theoretically I might be able to disengage myself from it, thanks to a miracle of some sort." [23]

Dino, afflicted with an excruciating boredom which results in a sense of futility, is simply not committed to the business of living. He is bored because his relationship with the world holds no meaning or value for him.

In a desperate effort to establish a relationship with

reality, to reach some kind of external definition, Dino engages in a love affair with a young model. The affair, carried to extreme limits, ends tragically as Cecilia leaves him and Dino attempts suicide. He is stung with jealousy when he discovers that Cecilia is unfaithful, but it is precisely at this point that he begins to "care" and to see Cecilia with new eyes. It is out of caring for Cecilia that Dino suffers, and it is this suffering that leads him to despair. Out of this anxiety he is brought back to life; he is frantic, longing, suffering; he is alive and involved, no longer bored.

The absurd lies behind this boredom; and behind the absurd lies death and nothingness. Dino attempts to cannibalize and introject the Other, to fill the void. The perfect solipsism of his relationship is shattered by separation; this partial detachment is for Dino the beginning of the existential I of the young model.

For Moravia, alienation exists and encompasses more than just man's withdrawal or inability to relate to the world at large. His characters do suffer greatly from their multidetermined outsidedness. This suffering, this dreadful loneliness or aloneness, becomes more terrible as the focus on Moravian "reality" is sharpened. This reality which will become one of the important aspects of subsequent analysis, is already seen as not only the human being or the human psyche, but the entire existential environment and the total world of nature.

It is true that Moravia's characters often give in to their alienation (refusal to suffer); that is, they choose to remain entrapped by their empty, hollow existence. For Moravia, alienation equals impotence. Too powerless to act, their indifference, futility, and frustration blind them to alternate courses of authentic conduct. But Moravia's men and women can also resolve their pointless suffering into acts which are meaningful, even though these very acts may bring further suffering. How-

ever, the difference just here between the varieties of
suffering is crucial: these new acts take on meaning and
purpose; they form the stuff of good faith and authenticity.

4

The Dualism of Moravian Sexuality

Since Freud, the word *sexuality* has become so abstract as to be almost free of a lucid connotation. Here we will reduce the focus in order to investigate its two ways, the "ambi-valence," as perceived by Alberto Moravia. These two valences are sexuality and death, and then sexuality and life. Two paths, the *Via Negativa* and the *Via Natura*, and their bifurcation. It is the purpose of this section to put this grand theme of Moravia's in an unequivocably existential context.

Setting our double-axis method to one side, we may begin with the truism that sex occupies the center of the literary stage for Alberto Moravia. But we have much to learn about this sex and whether his treatment of it makes him a great writer. Clearly the sensuous is the channel of the vital current between instinct and civilization, the channel that must be kept open for the individual, for the culture; this, we will see, amounts to a diagnosis on the part of the author. At the same time the sexual encounter is used as a very sharp literary tool to cut to the existential core of characters and their transactions. It, the sensual encounter, must be central in every major work because it is the model of the private limit situation. And from this paradigm everything, the exalted and the absurd, will be set before us to interpret. It is as if we imagined Moravia to say: "You have only

53

to redact a person's sexual behavior to 'know' them at every order of abstraction from the psychological autosphere to the political macrosphere." (Indeed, the link that Moravia forges between the carnal and the political is binding and irrestible.) So, sex (and we must now break this sex into its valences and pursue each axis home), sex is Moravia's core tool.

It is his tool but not, we think, his obsession. As we take up examples now of the pathosensual and the pansensual, a haunting apothegm from Tennessee Williams may provide a helpful formula, "the opposite of death is desire." [1]

Perhaps Moravia's major concept is the dialectic of conversion from "death" in life, to Life itself. This theme, which we here call conversion, is as important to Moravia as rebellion is to Camus. The existential life-change is central to both writers, but the problem is approached differently.

In *Luca*, an adolescent's physical yearnings bring him face to face with death. A seductive young governess has invited Luca to her apartment, but events do not materialize as he had imagined.

When the maid opened the door he was astonished at the pungent, stuffy smell from the hall that smote his face like a hot breath. The maid ushered him in and left him standing there. . . . the passage leading off the hall was plunged in darkness, and it seemed to him he could hear muffled sobs coming from that direction. The whole house seemed to be permeated by some inexplicable, sorrowful agitation—light, hurried footsteps, moans, rustling garments, creaking doors. . . . And the smell, the smell that was so pungent in his nostrils, was the smell of disinfectants, of sleep, of sweat; he remembered the same smell in his mother's room years ago during an illness. A tearful

voice close behind him made him start. "Who is it?
What do you want?" it said. . . . Mortified, he spoke
his own name, adding hurriedly the lie that he had
come to ask for news. The old woman muttered some
reply that Luca did not understand, ending with:
"She's sick—she's terribly sick." . . . He hurried
home. . . . he felt . . . hatred against . . . that
part of himself which had inflicted upon him the humiliation of that indecent chase across town; ending
in so mortifying a manner by his finding a death
agony where he had expected a lovers' meeting.[2]

This is stunning—"the opposite of death is desire."
Death and sexuality are clearly antipodal here and yet—
and this is the author's power of evocation—confluent.
The whole cross section is abstracted for us: smells,
sounds, memories of sick rooms past. The atmosphere is
medicinal, antiseptic, and at the same time packed with
sensory stimuli. Then, instead of the desirable governess
we are confronted with an old woman, a harbinger. Moravia rings changes on archetypes here. The road to
death leads not to old man Father Time, the road leads
through a young woman to her transformation as an old
hag. This is Freud's thesis—death is a woman! From her
generativeness to her decay, this conversion is the master
metaphor for death in this century. The woman, racially,
is the *genius loci* of existence and man, beyond the pleasure principle, is driven to enter her house of death by his
every instinct.

In a brief turn to the visual arts, this theme of sexuality and death is reflected in a startling parallel in the
work of Norwegian artist, Edvard Munch. He, too,
combines these same motifs into a single unified cycle.
Munch was able to transform his experience of woman
into a universal statement of the sexual-psychological
roles woman takes on in her affinity to man. This central

theme of woman's essential relationship to man is introduced in a series of paintings and prints called *The Sphinx*. Here, woman's function as a link in the chain of evolution—as the preserver of life and the carrier of death—calls forth images inherited from Nordic mythology. Physical love, for Munch, emerges as a basic antagonism between the sexes, leaving man trapped and enveloped by woman. This most basic of human relationships ultimately results in tragedy as seen in *Death and the Maiden*. Embryo and germinal cells surround the border of this print which depicts a young woman, who, in the act of creating life, is locked in the embrace of death. In Munch's imagery sexuality never approaches the sense of renewal or transformation which is found in Moravia's second equation: sexuality equals Life.

Sexuality and death are sharply equated by Moravia in a late novel, *The Lie*. Francesco Merighi, a journalist, is shocked to discover that his marriage has disintegrated. He sees his relationship as false and devoid of genuineness. Neither Francesco nor Cora desires to take the active step of separation; they agree to live in separate sections of the house and not invade the other's privacy.

Cora, who is a seamstress, has a second profession—that of a procuress. It is she who arranges for call girls to come to the house for Francesco's pleasure. When the first girl telephones, Francesco is doubtful, then he finds

> all of a sudden, to my surprise, I felt a profound and gloomy kind of excitement that seemed to derive both its justification and its force from the idea that the sex act was a thing of nullity and that all that was left to me now, in my present state of despair, was to plunge headlong into this nullity.[3]

For almost a year, Francesco engages in affairs of this type, thus putting into practice the idea of nihilism.

Moreover, I recognized that this was the case from the deathlike sensation I had every time I poured out my seed lovelessly upon these complaisant and unknown bodies. I would sink back . . . saying to myself: "I'm dying, yes I'm dying. I shall go on living, but I shall no longer be alive, ever again. I'm dying. I shall die and I shall not realize it and I shall continue to go about alive, but in truth I shall be dead." [4]

Finally, one sobering visit brings these affairs and this period of Francesco's life to an end. "One afternoon I was, as usual, expecting one of these many girls, a certain Gina, who had already been to my house on other occasions. But when I went to open the door I found myself face to face with a woman whom I did not know." [5] Fully clothed this very young girl gives the impression of a full, plump figure; once undressed, Francesco stares at her, astonished. "I saw in front of my eyes, not the soft, plump, childish female body I had pictured, but rather a skeleton covered with skin. . . . The only fleshy parts of her were her face, her neck, and her calves; all the rest was nothing but bones." [6] Curiously, Francesco inquires if being thin isn't a disadvantage in her job. With a certain air of conceit the girl replies that many men like her and want to see her again. "The other day there was a German. . . . He said he liked me better than any other girl he'd met here in Italy. He said something in German—wait a moment—*totentanz*. What does that mean?" [7] Francesco answers, "It means dance of death. . . . It was a painting they used to have in the churches. You could see Death dancing first with one person then with another—with a king, with a beggar, with a young man, with an old man . . . and so on. . . . It was intended to mean that death does not respect anybody, but carries them off, one and all. . . . That German was treating you as a skeleton, he was calling you Death." [8] Francesco reflects, "having gotten over my surprise, I had begun to feel a certain desire of, so to speak, an intellectual kind. Yes indeed, I thought, she was Death, the Death of the *danse macabre* in the church frescoes; but she was also that nullity which I had been hovering around for so long and which was at last presented to me in its true likeness. So I climbed on to the bed and threw myself with adequate force upon that pile of bones." [9]

Moravia's reference to a German is understandable, for we have come to regard Germany as the very symbol of depersonalization and alienation, sadism and the death wish itself. Strange stories from the war years reveal an endemically inverted sexuality shot through the social crimes with which we most conveniently charge the Germans. The existential diagnosis of those sexual anomalies, that comingle the erotic and murderous, would be that crimes against finitude (the body) may be seen at every level of action if only we would cease to categorize war, sex, politics as if they were not coeval at the deepest levels of Being. Other nations, too, reveal their sickness, and the public and the private symptoms appear, on closer scrutiny, to be merely two faces of the same disease. When man plays God he is, it seems, equally damned in all his circles.

It is this last experience of Francesco's which brings his past meaningless affairs sharply into focus. That he has actually been courting death—death personified in the skeletonlike figure of a young girl—is a frightening revelation. Sex, the act of nullity for him, is now seen as carrying nothingness to its logical end. Nothingness and death. As the girl leaves, Francesco reflects: "Death waved back at me and disappeared. The visit of the skeleton-girl marked the end of that period of my life. . . . Thus began a life which was entirely different from the life I had hitherto led." [10] This confrontation with death, this death-shock (the sexual act carried to extreme nullity), is that jarring event which brings about Francesco's conversion: the changing of his life.

Again, in *The Empty Canvas* an elderly painter's death wish is revealed in his obsessive physical desire for a young model. Dino relates the episode of Balestrieri's death.

> That same day, partly through the shocked allusions of the caretaker, partly through the more explicit comments of a group of friends whom I met at the café, I was able to reconstruct the old painter's end. It seemed that Balestrieri had died at a very special moment, that is, while he was in the act of making love with the girl who had so often smiled at me. . . . In reality Balestrieri had felt sick and had died under the frightened eyes of the girl; that was all that was known for certain. . . . On the other hand, in support of the "love-death" gossip, there was the reported statement of the doctor who had been summoned to the death bed: "If this man had realized that there are certain things that cannot be done at his age, he would still be alive." Others, however, maintained that, after examining Balestrieri, all the doctor had said to the girl was: "Signorina, you killed him," adding immediately afterwards: "Or rather, you helped him to kill himself." [11]

Later, when Dino acquires this Cecilia as a model, he begins to probe into the relationship between the young girl and Balestrieri. Cecilia is subjected to numerous cross-examinations concerning the affair.

> "Well then, tell me: in your opinion, did Balestrieri know that his relations with you were injuring his health?"
> "Yes, he did know."
> "What did he say?"

"He said: 'Some day or other this is going to kill me.' Then I told him that he ought to be careful, but he answered that it didn't matter. . . . Yes. . . . I remember one day when we were making love he said to me: 'Go on . . . even if I feel sick, I want you to make me die, yes, really to make me die.' "

". . . So you think he loved you because you made him die, I mean because for him you were a means he made use of to kill himself?" [12]

On another occasion Cecilia relates her last encounter with Balestrieri.

Yes, he used to want to make love at any moment, so to speak. We'd already done it once in the little room upstairs. . . . Suddenly he wanted to make love again, and he did it right there on the stairs. . . . After he felt sick, and I'd helped him to get upstairs to the bedroom again and onto the bed, he lay there for a little, with his eyes shut, quite still. Then gradually, he recovered—just imagine—he wanted to make love yet again, for the third time. [13]

Dino muses to himself, "So Balestrieri had really wished to kill himself. . . . I seemed to see those two, separating at the critical moment of their intercourse; and the old painter clinging with both hands to the banister and climbing up painfully, step by step, to the gallery and then going and falling on the bed; and then the corpse-like figure sitting up suddenly and holding out its arms to Cecilia." [14] Malraux's revolutionary, Kyo, approached his wife for the last time as though he were standing "before a death-bed." It is an old, old theme with a twentieth-century vengeance.

The inherent double meaning of the verb "to die" is the strongest kind of support for the author's grasp of sexual dualism. For seventeen hundred years the verb "to die" shared its descriptive-operative denotations with a universally popular signification: "to die" stood for sexual orgasm. (Shakespeare, for one, cannot be understood apart from this duality which reaches its maximum in Othello.) And folk language, like dream language, is wonderfully apophantic and metaphorical. A fascinating complexity provides us with real literary density when we remember that "to die" would also be an obligatory equivalent for a detumescence, for impotence of any kind. With the theme of *impotenza* the circle is complete. "To die" is joined to Moravia's other great idea, *impotenza*, and the overdetermined has become univocal; we are caught in a masterly web of unspeakable contiguities.

Now let us try to come home by another road. The sexual life axis in Moravia, when considered side by side with the death axis, seems to be not so much an antithesis as a synthesis, not really a simple positive but a transformation. This sexual life-axis, we believe, is not something untouched by death but rather is, itself, a victory over death—a victory produced by the most intimate contact or tension. Thus if life, at the biological level, heads straight for death, then Moravia's supersensuous bypath is a conversion, the illusion of a detour that really wends inexorably back toward the final crossroad. But without the illusion of this carnal new turning, Moravia seems to be saying, man lives like a beast.

In *Conjugal Love*, Moravia has written a love story of rare intensity. The novel dramatizes the conflict between intellect and instinct, a Moravian theme which presents itself over and over. Silvio Baldeschi is an intellectual young man who entertains pretensions of becoming a writer. His beautiful wife, Leda, is a woman strongly motivated by instinct. Silvio sees in her the attributes of a Greek goddess, mysterious and ethereal, at the same time splendid in her earthy attractiveness.

How often, as I lay beside her in bed, I contemplated her naked body and felt almost frightened at seeing it so beautiful, a beauty that even under my persevering gaze defied all definition! How often, as she lay there flat on her back with her head sunk in the pillow, I tousled and rearranged those long, soft, fair tresses of hers, seeking to understand the mysterious feeling of movement that gave them that fluttering, evasive look! How often I gazed at those enormous blue eyes of hers and wondered where lay the secret of their sweet, troubled expression! How often, after kissing her long and furiously, I analyzed the sensation my lips still retained, comparing it with the exact shape of *her* lips and hoping to penetrate the significance of that faint smile of almost archaic form which, after the kiss, became visible again at the corners of her big, sinuous mouth—precisely the smile that is to be seen in the earliest Greek statues. I had found a mystery as great—or so it seemed to me—as the mysteries of religion: a mystery close to my own heart, in which my eyes and my mind, well used to the examination of beauty, could lose themselves at last and find peace, as though in an enchanting, unlimited spaciousness. . . . I found my wife always ready and always docile, as though she were conscious of providing both herself and me with a reward and an outlet after so many hours of tranquility. In the rustic night that looked in through the wide-open windows, its deep silence broken only at rare intervals by the cry of a bird, in that dim and lofty room, our love would burst into sudden flame and burn long and silently, clear and living like the flame of the old oil lamps that once had illumined those sombre apartments. I felt that I loved my wife more each day, the feeling of each evening nourishing itself and gathering strength from that of the evening before; and she, on her side, seemed never to exhaust the treasure of her affectionate, sensual compliance. During those nights, for the first and, perhaps, the last time in my life, I seemed to grasp the meaning of what true conjugal passion can be—that mixture of violent devotion and lawful sensuality, of exclusive, limitless possession and confident joy in that possession.[15]

As Silvio describes their love making, sensuality is reminiscent of the life giving, nourishing powers of mother nature. Love, described here in terms of profound sexual intimacy, brings to life emotional and spiritual refreshment and strength.

Again there is a corresponding comparison with Italo Svevo's *As a Man Grows Older*. The difference here is that the lovers do not truly love each other. But it seems in this moment that Emilio touches on something universal, profound and compelling about the force of love.

He hastened to meet her and at the sight of her brilliant colouring, so strangely vivid, so flawless in its perfection, he felt his heart leap for joy within him . . . He had ventured timidly to caress her hair, which seemed to him so much pure gold . . . Like all who have never come into contact with the facts of life, he had believed himself stronger than the most exalted spirit, more indifferent than the most confirmed pessimist, and now he looked round him at the silent witnesses of this night's great event. The moon had not yet risen, but far out at sea an irridescent radiance hung upon the water as if the sun had but lately left it and everything were still reflecting its light . . . Everything seemed enormous and without boundary; the only thing which moved in that vast solitude was the colour of the sea. He felt that in the whole of nature at that moment he was the only active force, he alone was in love.

The two passages bear resemblance to one another although Silvio's love is an authentic feeling. Ironically, the cowardly and emotionally impoverished Emilio cannot really experience his love, and his feelings are nothing more than romanticized delusions. Nevertheless, these two writers capture the force of love through uniquely similar subjective world views.

In the novelette *Luca*, Moravia gives us one of the most moving, exalted examples of the sexuality that brings life. Luca's progressive withdrawal from the world brings about a severe illness which culminates in a conscious death wish. An initiation into sexual experience leads him finally and irrevocably back to life.

It was not so much an embrace he experienced as a sinking of the whole of himself in a limitless expanse of flesh. . . . he had the precise feeling that she was . . . introducing him, a reverent novice, into a mysterious cave dedicated to a religious rite. This, he thought, was the life he had formerly invoked. . . . Filled with gratitude, he found himself kissing the thin brown face with the closed eyes, motionless as an effigy. But was it the face of the nurse, or that of some deity risen up from the earth for his possession? . . . Meanwhile the sense of relief continued, and, with its freshness and buoyancy, redeemed the ardor and the gravity of the embrace. The nurse went away next day . . . Luca was left with a feeling neither of regret nor disgust, but rather of gratitude for his final initiation not merely into physical love but also into that more general love for all things. . . . He felt he had at last found a new and quite personal way of looking at reality—a way that was composed of sympathy and patient expectation. . . . Now . . . he would see things first with those new eyes which had opened that night inside him. . . . Second and truer mother, the nurse had given him a second birth when, in his desire for death, he had been already dead. But he knew that this second birth could never have taken place if he had not first desired, so sincerely, so wholeheartedly, to die.[16]

Later, he seeks to define the truest, deepest meaning of this experience.

He remembered that at the moment of the embrace he had felt a sudden, strong desire to enter completely, with the whole of his body, into the woman's belly, and curl up there, in that warm, rich darkness, just as he had lain curled up before he was born. But now he understood that the womb was nothing else than the womb of life itself, hitherto repudiated by him but which the woman, imperiously, had compelled him to accept. Yes, he concluded, that is what life should be: . . . a dark, cavern of loving, maternal flesh into which he could enter confidently, sure that he would be protected there as he had been protected by his mother all the time she was carrying him in her womb. Life meant the sinking of oneself in this flesh and feeling its darkness, its engulfing power, its convulsion, to be beneficent, vital things. Suddenly he understood the significance of the sense of relief that had refreshed him while the nurse was crushing him in her embrace.[17]

With great sensitivity, Moravia has given us a profound insight into man's sexuality. Luca's experience has not only redeemed his life, but his manhood as well. The mysterious sense of trust and confidence which accompanied the sinking into maternal flesh has expanded itself to embrace the whole of life. Luca's heightened responsiveness has invoked a new way of looking at reality; a fuller, calmer way, enlarged by compassion and trust. Life is a "broad, swirling, powerful stream. . . . and closing his eyes, he abandoned himself to it trustfully, as he had abandoned himself a few days before in the arms of the nurse." [18]

The existential Moravia lays on hands, quite literally, and this confuses very astute critics like R. W. B. Lewis who draws an unfortunate conclusion from his reading of the particularly kinesthetic novella, *Luca*.[19] Luca is an adolescent from the upper middle class. He is nursed during his breakdown by a woman whose final loving gesture is sexual. Luca is returned from non-Being to Being between the timeless thighs of the nurse (she has called forth the tumescence of Being; he has followed his own trajectory into the "dark, unplumbable" depths of nature; he is left exhausted on the other side—life). Here the critic calls the act a recovery that is isolated, private, and "metaphysical"; but Moravia, unlike Camus or Malraux, is content to end his stories short of a moral code. His point is that the discovery (not recovery), the healing, is physical; its metaphysical vicissitudes are left implicit. The nurse is the agency of wholeness, her body is healing, holy. Time after time the protagonists are brought to a new relationship with reality, not by, but *through* the woman and the act.

To pursue the figure, non-Being must be left in the woman. Moravia confirms this by refusing to substitute the appropriate diction for his own voice when he has Adriana, the prostitute of his great common novel *Woman of Rome*, soliloquize before going to sleep. She has just been filled with the non-Being of a revolutionary who is in bad faith, who tells her he has "died forever." In Moravia's voice she thinks:

I began to think about the sea again and was overcome by the longing to drown myself. I imagined it would only be a moment's suffering, and then my

lifeless body would float from wave to wave beneath
the sun for ages. The gull would peck my eyes, the
sun would burn my breast and belly, the fish would
gnaw my back. At last I would sink to the bottom,
would be dragged head downwards towards some icy
blue current that would carry me along the sea bed
for months and years among submarine rocks, fish
and seaweed, and floods of limpid salt water would
wash my forehead, my breast and my belly, my legs
slowly wearing away from my flesh, smoothing and
refining me continually. And at last some wave would
cast me up on some shore, nothing but a handful of
fragile, white bones . . . and perhaps someone without noticing it would walk on my bones and crush
them to white powder. With these sad, voluptuous
thoughts, I fell asleep.[20]

This woman of Rome has been called by suspicious
critics one of the author's few "healthy" creations. Yet,
certain images leap out from the page; an extraordi-
narily revealing and carnal vision is projected through
the sea imagery that Moravia manipulates so effortlessly;
for he is a Mediterranean, a man of the *Midi*. This
fantasy does not show us the critics' Adriana with her
dirty glamour, her mythic whore-goddess wisdom or her
insightful street psychology. What we do find is masoch-
ism, guilt, punishment, and the craving alternately for
transubstantiation and non-Being, nothingness. The
rebel *manqué* lying by her side has filled our quondam
critical fertility symbol with alienation, angst, bad faith,
even a fascism of visceral sorts. The economy of the
transaction with reality, with nature as mediator, is not
simple for Moravia any more than it was for Kazantzakis. The almost mythic Greek, whose life was in great
part devoted to the understanding of the transformations of matter into spirit, resembles the Italian in the

belief that the sense of identity—between beings through sexuality in all its dimensions—is contagious. Adriana is unquestionably a great soul as created, but her maker, too, is extraordinary in never flinching from the risks of an existential identity resembling his heroine's. She, as prostitute, is a slate that registers the mark of each client and then, by natural sleep and an act of will, is free to make contact with the next. Her pregnancy, like Lena Groves's in *Light in August*, is a victory over non-Being and Moravia does not hesitate to use the powerful symbol when a coup is required. Adriana, like Kazantzakis's Jesus, feels the seductive agony of death and nonexistence running into her body. From the physical to the metaphysical, from birth to rebirth, from existence to essence—these are the stations of existential salvation.

How much greater the suffering of our day seems. In this madness of our convulsive time span, sexuality is asked to bear an evolutionary burden that has brought the pursuers of *la dolce vita* to grief. Moravia prophetically reaches beyond the pleasure principle when he pits the death wish against the nature of sexuality. The struggle is an unequal one and every resulting anomaly is guaranteed. The ambience of world-weariness and flesh-horror so easy to sense in the purity of the Italian's prose is inevitable, given his existential decision to accept the closing of all ecstatic doors save one, and that a hole that leads back to nature or on to complete nihilism, to Being or nonbeing.

In *Luca*, sexuality is symbolized, in the old way, as Mother Nature, that powerful force which not only initiates life, but which subsequently nurtures life and brings fulfillment and enlarges its very meaning. Moravia has an extraordinary grasp of essential transformation: "Filled with gratitude, he found himself kissing the thin brown face with the closed eyes"; the mother-

nurse is also "some deity risen up from the earth"—
death itself. But there is no hint of moral necrophilia,
only the sexual boundary situation, the radical vacilla-
tion from life to death, forcing the body to choose. The
nurture of sexual union is its rebirth. Mother-nature and
mother-death plus the carnal presence and "friendship"
of the nurse of the moment—these are the three women
of Luca; his fateful, faithful sisters.

At first glance Moravia would appear to be far more
obsessed with the needs of the body than the needs of
the spirit. The sexual appetite is one valid way of
measuring man's humanity. He knows this and uses
this method to good advantage. But he is equally aware
that this is not the only vocabulary for explaining human psychology. Exposure to only a few of his short
stories instructs us that Moravia utilizes many other
instincts and emotions. Greed, lust, selfishness, love,
depravity, narcissism, jealousy; in short, all the attributes
or potentialities of the human psyche act as the raw
material for his journey into the human condition. Indeed, the more we scrutinize Moravia, the more he con-
vinces us that *all* instincts and emotions have the
potential of revealing something instructive, meaningful
and distinct about man's nature and therefore about
man himself. At the existential level, there is only
energy.

In ending a discussion of sexuality it is instructive to
let Moravia speak for himself. In the essay "Eroticism in
Literature," he makes a distinction between eroticism
in pagan and modern literature. Eroticism springs directly from nature in pagan literature. It has all the
innocence, coarseness, and cohesion that modern literature lacks. Modern literature must grapple with the
Christian experience and with the sense of sin that
divides and turns nature against itself. "With the pa-
gans, freedom was an unconscious, simple fact, whereas

with the moderns it has been reclaimed, rediscovered, rewon. In compensation eroticism in modern literature has, or should have, the character proper to subjects that neither shock nor draw undue attention to themselves—that are, in short, normal if we understand normal to mean the transformation of the sexual act into something scientifically known and poetically valid, and therefore insignificant from the ethical point of view." [21]

Moravia feels that the sexual act can now, for the first time since the pagan literatures, be represented directly, poetically, and realistically without the need for sign, symbols, and metaphoric disguises. But *must* a writer deal with the sexual encounter and, if so, when? "My answer is that it is not always necessary to talk about the sexual act, just as it is not always necessary to talk about social questions or adventures in Africa, but that, as the prohibitions and taboos that stood in its way no longer exist today, to pass it over in silence when it *is* necessary is no longer, as it once was, a moral question but an inadequacy of expression." [22]

Few will deny that modern literature is characterized by a rather marked predilection to talk about the sexual act. For Moravia the reason for this is simply "that in the modern world sex is synonymous with love, and who could deny that love is a very common subject in the literatures of all times and places?" [23]

He further observes that taboos and prohibitions were the probable outcome of a slow social involution and that the most important factor in their collapse was depth psychology or psychoanalysis. He understands that the discoveries of psychoanalysis have had a crucial result in two ways: they have broken down the taboos, and have raised the sexual act from the ignominy into which the taboos had cast it and have reinstated it among the few ways of expression and communion available to man.

The sexual act in modern literature is . . . as it shows itself when we manage to separate it both from moralistic horror and vulgar hedonism: an act of insertion into a cosmic and superhuman order. Seen in this way the sexual act is effectively something higher, more mysterious, and more complete than love, especially if love is interpreted as the simple physico-sentimental relationship between man and woman.[24]

We have quoted at some length in order to underscore the great persistence of the interdicting themes of death and sexuality, the dual radicals of existence. Moravia, perhaps more than anyone since Chekov, even more than Thomas Mann, goes beyond the psychological toward the supersensuous. He is the artist as physician, and the cathartic exegesis he provides for his protagonists' crisis is definitive twentieth-century writing.

5

The Absurd

Before beginning a discussion of how the absurd reveals itself in the writing of Moravia, the term itself should be considered. A brief semantic journey seems not only pertinent but necessary. The term "absurd" has caught on, and in catching on it has become muddied and imprecise as to its broader, fuller meaning in existential thought. In one sense it has become more precise and associated with only one category of art.

The absurd has most recently become the exclusive property of the drama or the theatre. A certain group of dramatists have given themselves over to depicting the absurdities of the human condition; so much so that their plays have even merited the name "theatre of the absurd." It is as if by extolling the absurd (here "absurd" in its purest form, meaning only inconsistency with western logic, contrary to reason, or ridiculously incongruous) these dramatists intend to force man to examine his ways. Until man recognizes the absurdity of his plight, he cannot aspire to a meaningful solution. So a theatre of ideas seems to be discarded in favor of a more urgent, more primary, though nonetheless dramatic, statement: man is a mad animal. It is as if the modern dramatist were saying, Recognize this, then we can begin to build! But, it is apparent that this message is univocal in all the varying forms of serious modern thought, rational as well as nonrational. Brecht's "you who only stare now, learn to see" expresses the alarm and the current eschatology admirably. If there is a consensus concerning message among such widely disparate stylists as Beckett and Brecht—the two giants of the twentieth-century drama—then it must be the ritualistic vocabulary that each employs idiosyncratically along with the absurd lexicon of Ionesco, Pinter and the others.

"Je ne capitulerai pas!" I will not capitulate! is Berenger's credo, hurled hopelessly at the proliferating rhinos.[1] This Ionescan cry is another way of abstracting absurd drama. But Ionesco is a linguistic poet, while Beckett is a silence man and Brecht a didactic magician. The vision of the absurd is Kazantzakis's "Cretan glance —without hope but without fear," and yet there is always the rumor of Hope whenever a putative Prometheus is on the scene, or Berenger, or the creature from *Endgame* who, on his hands and knees, defies Hamm with "mad eyes," or most of all Brecht's Schweikean rebels who whisper "no" under their breath. These are all modern and absurd Prometheans, or rather, their authors are. They, like the first fire-bringers, allow Hope to escape from her bag of evils so that man will dare, will be able to bear to live. "An absurd world," says Camus, "where even the moles dare to hope."

It is the absurd in this narrow, pure sense, as exemplified in drama, that we are trying to get away from in the case of Moravia. To trace the role of the absurd in the existential context, it seems pertinent to start with Kierkegaard. Before beginning, a word of caution must be injected. To dismiss such thinkers as Kierkegaard, Camus, Malraux, and Sartre in a few sentences will be offensive to many readers. However, it must be borne in mind that we are dealing with their thought only in a very restricted area—the absurd—and this will be further boiled down to its barest essentials. No attempt is being made to relate the absurd and its ramifications to the larger philosophical formulation of each of these writers. It is the evolution of "absurd" in the existential context that needs to be briefly clarified.

The word (whose meaning, ironically, suggests deafness, silence, and cacophony at the same time) enters the modern vocabulary of ideas with Kierkegaard. Stripped of other meanings and intricacies, the word absurd means the very nature of life for Kierkegaard. Absurdity equals God. God becomes impossible, belief becomes impossible without recognizing this absurdity. Kierkegaard gives the example of Abraham sacrificing his son, Isaac. This absurd command of God is one which Abraham cannot question, he must believe. He accepts the absurdity of killing his son and both are spared. He cannot question the command as he cannot question God. By accepting the absurdity of killing his son, he is saved. For that very great man, Kierkegaard, the leap toward Jesus and transcendence was ludicrous, absurd, and *therefore* a call to meaning and a victory over death. Dostoyevsky, too, used a saviour as the makeweight of his reality and in his devastating and perversely comic statement, "Between the truth and Jesus Christ, I choose Jesus Christ," he reveals the joke of faith; a joke that one must die for if necessary. In the twentieth century the word, stripped of much of its nineteenth-century Messianism, reenters the language with Andre Malraux and his call for "anguish and radical solidarity" as a new version of the social contract. Was God there, or had Nietzsche's revolutionary categorical imperative supplanted Him? Nietzsche had taught that because man was impotent, unwatched, lonely, lost, guilty, fearful, base, megalomaniacal, a child and a poseur, in short, because man was absurd no crime was permitted against him; that his precarious survival—physically, psychologically, morally—forbids any outrage against him. Certainly Camus and Kazantzakis are Zarathustra's sons, and it is with Camus that the absurd

finds its philosophical definition. It should be stated
parenthetically here that the French neoclassic tradition
has given us another vision of the absurd. Unlike
Ionesco's and Beckett's divergent imitations of the unspeakable, the brilliant and lucid modern French theatre
is gloriously literary but nonetheless obsessed with
meaning and therefore with the absurd. Unlike Ionesco,
it is from Camus's *Théâtre de l'equipe* and his *Théâtre
du Travail* that the French drama of the absurd ema-
nates. The roots are the pagan and Christian myths of
the Greeks and at the same time the master "novel" of
Dostoyevsky's New Testament. A glance at the titles
of this French investigation of truth (the absurd) reveals
how radically different are the two strategies for coming
at meaning: *Caligula, Electra, The Flies, The Possessed,
Antigone, The Infernal Machine, Tiger at the Gates,
Waiting for Godot*, too, was written in French, and
The Lesson, but language for these latter has come to
a stop.

It is Camus, then, who gives us, typically, the sublime
figure of Sisyphus as our talisman in the world. It is the
"project" of Sisyphus, to use Sartre's term, to roll a
stone up a mountain slope only to watch it time and
again crash back down to the base or beginning of the
ascension. Sisyphus, in common with the other great
rebels, has stolen God's secrets, and for this worst of all
crimes he is, by the law of the talion, condemned to the
worst of all punishments: the futile life task of shoulder-
ing a stone toward an endemic, inexorable fall; he is
condemned to absurdity. And yet this absurd punishment—life itself—yields, after much suffering, a strange
joy that both Camus and Moravia seem to understand
best.

I leave Sisyphus at the foot of the mountain! One
always finds one's burden again. But Sisyphus teaches
the higher fidelity that negates the gods and raises

rocks. He too concludes that all is well. This universe henceforth without a master seems to him neither sterile nor futile. Each atom of that stone, each mineral flake of that night-filled mountain, in itself forms a world. The struggle itself toward the heights is enough to fill a man's heart. One must imagine Sisyphus happy.[2]

Finally, Moravia seems to derive his grammar of the absurd from two major sources: the doomsday statistics of this century and his own wartime exile. From the now hundreds of millions of corpses that the German University, the French Dictionary, the English Parliament, and, most ominous of all, the American Dream, have produced—with their Enlightenment, Reason, Ratiocination, and Progress—Moravia has inhaled the stench of death itself and the infection of the absurd. During the occupation, when as a fugitive, Moravia lived a sad and bestial exile, starving in a mountain hut, much was revealed to him. The precocious cosmopolitan died and was reborn as the lucid, passionate beholder of the absurd, against which he rebels and is joyful.

When we examine the meaning of the absurd for Moravia, we find this meaning suffused in the total human condition. Absurdity reflects itself in the totality of life. But what is this totality? Moravia's view is not expanded into a complicated metaphysical framework, with God at its center, as is Kierkegaard's. The totality of life for Moravia is man himself; it is man who is ridiculous and absurd. Further, man reveals his absurdity in his relationship to other men. More specifically, it is man's inhumanity to man which becomes the thematic vehicle Moravia uses to reveal man in all his ambiguity and absurdity. Life (man), in this absurdity, is a spoilsport; it is always doing us in, it is out to get us.

Absurdity equals suffering. It is man who suffers

because of the absurdity of his life. This capacity for suffering is what separates man from animal. In *Man as an End*, Moravia says, "This suffering is the proof that man can only be an end, indeed the only possible end, and that—whatever the efforts made—he will never become a means. The whole texture of the modern world is formed of this suffering. It finds expression in the ugliness of cities, the stupidity of amusements, the brutality of love, the slavery of work, the ferocity of wars, the decay of the various arts to the level of palliatives, propaganda and flattery. It is manifest in all man's activities. Indeed it is the frame on which the whole fabric of modern civilisation is spun." [3]

There is no more explicit example of modern man's suffering than the tragic events of the first half of this century. Two world holocausts and extermination camps brought infinite suffering and immense destruction on mankind. Moravia sees the absurdity of the modern world reflected in the death wish—"a longing for death and destruction and dissolution that may well be the last spasm of the great suicidal orgy of the two world wars." [4] To Moravia, the modern world is a "perfectly organised nightmare." [5] He sees this characteristic exemplified in all recent literature. Furthermore, both pessimism and optimism inspire a feeling of suffocation and claustrophobia. "In varying ways all modern poetry expresses this feeling of suffocation. Whether by affirmation or denial it warns men: the modern world is absurd." [6]

In this same work, *Man as an End*, which was written at the end of World War II, Moravia dwells at length on the modern state as it has evolved in Nazi Germany and Fascist Italy. "The modern State, whose end is the State and whose means is man, is a nightmare of such gigantic proportions that the man who lives inside of the nightmare is probably as unaware of it as an ant crawling on a tree is unaware that it is a tree. . . . In the modern world we know . . . that the use of man as the means lies at the origin of the feeling of absurdity and nightmare that the world itself inspires." [7] Moravia feels that modern man has lost the sense of his own sacred character; or rather the dark awareness or suspicion that man is a man. If man could clarify or define this suspicion, he "would cease to be a means and become an end again." [8]

Years earlier Svevo spoke of the absurdity of modern man's predicament; the condition that Moravia would use as his obsession. At the end of *The Confessions of Zeno*, the war becomes the concrete, universal symbol which points to final absurdity. Zeno, who profits from the war, is able to observe that "our life is poisoned to the root." Thinking himself cured, Zeno abandons his psychoanalysis. But ironically his last thoughts reflect his hopeless capitulation to doom.

But spectacled man invents implements outside his body, and if there was any health or nobility in the inventor there is none in the user. Implements are bought or sold or stolen, and man goes on getting weaker and more cunning. It is natural that his cunning should increase in proportion to his weakness. The earliest implements only added to the length of his arm, and could not be employed except by the exercise of his own strength. But a machine bears no relation to the body. The machine creates disease because it denies what has been the law of creation throughout the ages. The law of the strongest disappeared, and we have abandoned natural selection. We need something more than psychoanalysis to help us. Under the law of the greatest number of machines, disease will prosper and the diseased will grow ever more numerous. [9]

Zeno despairs of his existence and gives in to dark suspicions and ominous speculations. But for the Moravian man, these terrible suspicions, which are now a reality, provide the fuel for his existence. His being is challenged and he will fight back. The fact that he may not, or cannot, win is superfluous. What matters is the engagement; the essential act even in an absurd environment. As long as there is life he must struggle against absurdity.

That Moravia suffered under the stifling political climate of fascist Italy there can be no doubt. His writing, a flagrant opposition to fascist mythology, was eventually banned. For a short time he wrote under a pseudonym but even this had to stop. He became involved in antifascist journalism which ended abruptly when the Germans occupied Rome. From a magazine interview we learn something of this difficult period of his life. "In 1943, when the Fascist regime fell and the Germans occupied the country I had to flee to avoid being arrested. I fled with my wife into the mountains. From September to May, we lived in a pigsty on top of a mountain near Cassino. It was very cold and there was no food, and so on. There was terrible bombing all the time. Soon after the Americans arrived—the Fifth Army —I came back to Rome." [10]

This exile in the mountains—living like an animal in a desperate effort to accomplish the most basic of all human needs, survival—must have revealed itself to Moravia as the act of extreme absurdity that, indeed, it was. His writer's sensibility could not help but be affected by these nine months of hideous boredom and discomfort and inactivity. It is surely out of this experience that Moravia fashioned an account of living in a hut which occurs in a story in *More Roman Tales*.

Have you ever lived in a hut? No; and so you know nothing at all about huts. . . . Living in a hut means that, if it rains, you have to be careful where you put your feet when you get out of bed in the morning, because there is mud all over the floor. It means cooking in a petrol tin, out of doors, and sitting on the bed to eat. It means using a carbide lamp or a candle for lighting. . . . It means huddling together like beasts to keep warm, and fighting with draughts and dampness all through the winter. And then you can never find anything, in a hut. You look for a fork, you look for a piece of soap, you look for the frying-pan, and out pops some other thing that you haven't any need of—a shoe, a cap or quite possibly a black, shaggy rat as big as a cat. . . . One night I heard strange chirping sounds coming from a box full of rags which I kept under the bed; I went and looked, and there amongst the rags I found eight little pink rats which looked like so many tiny little pigs. Well, I killed them; but what fault was it of theirs? Huts are places for rats, not for human beings.[11]

In depicting the absurdities of human nature, Moravia can, at rare times, do so with the skill of a polished comedian. A distinction must be made regarding Moravia's humor. He is seldom "funny," and in those instances when he does display humor it is most always cloaked with the heavy veil of irony. His humor is never free or relaxed; it never exists for its own sake. There must always be a mixture of the sad, the ironic, the poignant with the comic. Interestingly, Moravia has said, "My greatest ambition is to write a comic book but it's the most difficult thing of all."

This Moravian humor is revealed in a story from *The Fetish* which relates the absurdity of a young girl's actions. Here a family is in a state of disintegration and decline. The children are all leaving home for work or school and the eldest daughter is about to be married.

Leonora is not marrying for love but out of convenience: "Economic necessity seemed to . . . be a good justification." [12] The suitor, Moroni, is a gross, vulgar, horrible young man, but he has the one advantage of being wealthy. There is a description of him which is one of the most remarkable descriptions Moravia has written of any character. Aside from being very funny, it must be included for its sheer brilliance.

> Moroni was not tall but rather massive, with a short neck and broad shoulders. His hair was thick and black, his eyes prominent, brown, bright but devoid of expression, his complexion muddy, his nose stumpy, crooked-looking from in front and aquiline in profile. It was his mouth, particularly, that Leonora disliked: thick but shapeless, it made one think of a full purse. And full, in fact, it was, of large, close-set teeth which overlapped and encroached upon each other as though he had a double or triple row of teeth like a shark. [13]

How like Moravia to convey the fact of the young man's wealth in a facial description—the mouth resembling a full purse! Moroni proceeds to tell Leonora about his family and himself, even his defects. He admits to being dictatorial, full of prejudices, and egotistical. Leonora reflects to herself: "He's a monster, I'm marrying a monster." [14] She begins to joke with Moroni and tells him she is not going to marry him. Finally, out of resignation, indifference, and loyalty to family she accepts the young man. The story ends.

> She was aware that these were the last days of her family life; and her heart sank. And, knowing that she had a faithful nature, she would be a good wife to Moroni, even if she did not love him; and thus, by force of circumstances, she would be led to become his associate. She would bear him children, she would

share his ideas, she would defend his conduct. Her heart trembled as she thought of all these things, her hand resting on the door-handle. Then she plucked up courage and went in.[15]

This young girl's acceptance of her fate out of obedience to parental wishes ends the story on a disquieting and depressing note. Loyalty to family is equated to loyalty to husband; but this loyalty is entirely negative. Leonora has become a commodity to be used. She will be used by her husband as she has been by her family. She will suffer because of this marriage; but this suffering will be unmeaningful, it will not be borne out of or for love. Leonora's suffering, evolving from an absurd, unloving act, will become the extreme absurdity. For, according to Moravia, it is only through love that man suffers meaningfully. Leonora's is an intimate fascism. Moroni was to seduce all Italy and loyalty was to be his song. This story is, in many ways, a rehearsal for European history. Once again the sexual is an abstraction of the political. Moravia is a master in this sphere.

In a story from *More Roman Tales*, a man's absurd actions have a far different effect. Serafino loses his girl to an aggressive young tough. The pair inflict verbal and physical abuse, then run off, leaving Serafino in the gutter. Sobbing, and feeling very lonely, he gets up and starts on his way.

At that moment I was crossing Via Principessa Clotilde, a street full of advertisement hoardings through which no one ever passes; goodness knows why they stick up posters there. And then, as I saw a row of these posters, all just the same, advertising some kind of soap, with a huge picture of a film actress saying she washed her face with this soap every day, I had a sudden impulse to write. . . . so I took a stump of pencil out of my pocket and . . . inspired by hatred towards women, who now seemed to me to be all of

them like Clementina, I gave the actress a pair of
moustaches and a goatee beard in the Victor Em-
manuel style. Then, still sobbing, I wrote in the blank
space: "You ugly, vile slut, to betray me with a crook
like Rosario. Very well, when the Russians come, we'll
see about it." I wrote some more abuse of Clementina
on two other posters; on a fourth I wrote: "Rosario,
scum of Rome, dirty swindler;" and gradually, as I was
writing, I realized I had stopped sobbing, and little by
little I felt better, more and more relieved. . . . At
the far end of Via Principessa Clotilde there was still
one poster left: I gave the actress a moustache again
and then turned back towards the Piazzale Flaminio,
feeling as light as air and almost completely comforted.[16]

Here the jilted lover has suffered a terrible blow to his
ego (I); his narcissism has been hurt. He overcomes his
painful feelings, these holes in his identity, by spiteful
action. Moravia shows us the therapeutic value of the
irrational. Every option is exhausted under the absurd.

Life is absurd, humorous, and treacherous, filled with
the deceits men play upon one another. But the recognition of an absurd universe does not have to end in
despair. For with this recognition begins the leap, the
struggle to build and to create meaning. Rejection of
this struggle, says Camus, would logically end in suicide.
Thus Sisyphus is happy because he has conquered despair. The answer to the riddle of life must come from
the depths of the individual conscience, must be sought
within the self and not the world and its categories.
Meaning is centrifugal from the I.

Moravia would not have us sickened unto death by
the reality of absurdity. But, therapeutically, this recognition, and the strength to grapple with it, should bring
us one step further toward fulfillment and self-knowl-
edge.

6

Nihilism and Crime

It is, perhaps, a puzzle why the literature, if not the life, of the modern age should be defined by crime and the criminal. Tolstoy and Dostoyevsky are cardinal examples, but Sartre and Moravia are very much a part of this tradition. True, there is hardly any phenomenon to exemplify megalomania and vanity as well as crime (unless it be gratuitous martyrdom or patriotism), and Sartre, in dubbing Genet a saint, is expressing a value and a metaphor for commitment and for a project. And yet a deeper reflection reminds us that crime and natural disaster have always been key literary devices. The incest and parricide of Oedipus are the source of the plague that is decimating Thebes, while Claudius's crime in *Hamlet* renders the whole state of Denmark "rotten." In the modern version, by contrast, everyman's crime creates only subterranean echoes. The cosmos, the State, and the individual are no longer inextricable functions of each other and when alienated, aliatory, underground metropolitan man knows sin, the stunning horror is that nothing changes perceptibly. He must suffer in silence; his institutions are immune to the tossing of his life, his own mate or family guesses nothing until it is too late. The revolution of modern literature is that sin has become invisible, anonymous, and evil has become banal.

Tragedy and great comedy have always involved crime

and punishment. Why? The idea of sin (crime) demands closure, completion. Structurally, all problem solving could be said to be modeled on the detective story. At a lower level of involvement, the mystery provides suspense and strong vicarious satisfaction, but at the highest order we experience something sacred. Since, in true art, we know in advance who the agent of evil is (recognition rather than cognition) we identify all the more closely with the protagonist. In great art the hero is the law-breaker, while in mere entertainment the hero is the lawmaker who destroys the rebel. The point being that ratiocination is a kind of sleuthing for clues that will finally add up to a new construct, while the more total cathartic involvement of important literature is a search or strategy that puts revelation and the disclosure of one's own identity in the place of suspense and moralism.

Nietzsche in the "Pale Criminal" differentiates with aphoristic lucidity between the crime, the idea of the crime, and the buried impulse toward the crime, and insists that "the wheel of casuality doth not roll between them." [1] This means that the deed itself, the crime, is not simply the extension of the image or the impulse, else we would all be overt criminals! And yet in our dreams and hearts, say the great writers, we all gratify our sorest needs at the expense of the world and reality, and this is metaphysical crime! But the legal criminal goes over the line and attacks the world and the sphere of other people's influence, and it is this collision of the socially real and the metaphysically, criminally real that provides us with the Iagos, the Emma Bovarys, the Roskolnikovs, the Caligulas, together with the most radical revelation of the intensity of needs from which the crime has grown. Not the *reason* for the act but the intensity —that is the purpose of art; it gives us structure and media (transactions) in terms of intensity, not in plots and props. Thus we know before the play begins, the argument and upshot of any great work—from *Oedipus the King* to *Waiting for Godot*. Crime, by seeming to be the most unreasonable of acts, is bound to tell us most concerning the human condition in all of its nonrational, ontological unspeakability. For crime, like life, there are no reasons, only pretexts. Then what better summary or symbol for life than crime?

We have only to read a few selections from any short-story collection to discover that Moravia's world is infested with murderers, whores, beggars, petty thieves, bums; in truth, a sad assortment of disreputable underworld types. But this world of crime—of nihilism—is not always the nihilism of unlawful death and destruction; it is one of moral nihilism as well. Nihilism just as often formulates itself around the clash between conventional ethics or society and the individual Being or instinct.

One facet of Moravian nihilism which emerges over and over again is cruelty—man's monstrosity toward man. This hypersensitivity to the cruelty of existence is not a melancholy attitude; Moravia knows it exists, and lived it for nine months in a filthy mountain cave. Further, cruelty is not the exclusive or sacred right of the few; there are no Hitlers or Mussolinis who corner the market on cruelty; but rather cruelty runs rampant, leaving no one exempt—it belongs to all of us. It is not reserved for those in positions of power; cruelty infects the lowest of men. The stupidity of cruelty pervades the entire sociological structure. It becomes a common, predictable, everyday occurrence. We are confronted with the generic descendents of Dostoyevsky's man from underground. The city! The locus of the louse, the modern nightmare scenario drawn up so long ago in the Haymarket of St. Petersburg.

Moravia displays unflinching courage in showing us as we are. He does not, out of charity or sentimentality, turn his eyes from the terrible truths of human atavism. Nihilism, then, in its many macabre and violent aspects, is used unsparingly by Moravia. But why is this so? Certainly he means to do more than mirror the crime and violence which confronts us daily in the newspaper headlines. We hope to prove that Moravia's use of crime goes beyond this mirror image to reasons more fundamental and provocative. In courageously dealing with the morbid, Moravia is able to make sense of life; he leaps over the nihilism to give life meaning. Like Faulkner, he dwells on the atavistic out of horror and counterphobia, not from any fascination.

Once again, we must look to the theme of conversion which is so important to the total vision of Moravia—that conversion which implies and reveals the value of living and for which one changes one's beliefs and sublimates one's loyalties. His characters fight their way out of sickness and death in order to center on a renewed sense of life. This conversion, though often agonizing, is wholeheartedly given over to the act of living. The reason for life must be extorted from the abyss of nihilism. Any contemporary writer, if he is to make an authentic or relevant statement, must use as a starting point the nihilism reflected in the world around him.

Nihilism, as we know it since Dostoyevsky's literally lousy *Homo Metropolitan* first peered out from under the floorboards, is a plague spread on the *Zeitgeist* of men by two media: war and the city. War and the city hang over Moravia's little worlds as surely as they interpenetrate his big worlds, depending on the idiom of the particular story.

The city, Rome, and its psychology are Moravia's métier; existentialism is, in its modern sense, a strategy of the city. The city is media, a madhouse of change. Moravia is a cosmopolitan in a very different way from Dostoyevsky, his nineteenth-century influence.

"Peasants don't know about anything except the land, they are ignorant and they live like beasts." He started laughing, and answered: "Some time ago it wouldn't have been a compliment, but today it is. Today it's the people who read and write and live in towns and are gentlefolk who are the really ignorant, the really uncultivated, the really uncivilized ones. With them there's nothing to be done, but with you peasants one can begin from the very beginning." I did not quite understand what he meant: "What d'you mean, beginning from the very beginning?" "Well," he said, "making new men of them." "It's quite clear," I exclaimed, "that you don't know anything about peasants, my dear boy. With peasants, there's nothing to be done. Why, what d'you think peasants are? They're the oldest people in the world. New men, indeed! They were peasants before anyone else existed, long before there were people in towns. They are peasants and they will always be peasants." [2]

One is left with ambivalence toward city and country; the hopes and sentiments of Dostoyevsky and Tolstoy have been rudely dissipated in Moravia's secure irony. City man is not an invidious comparison to rustic man; they have both been leveled by the times.

In another place Moravia, as if remembering his brutish wartime exile, seems to warn us.

How often have I thought that a human being has the right to be treated as a human being and not as a beast, and that treating a human being as such means giving him the opportunity to keep clean, in a clean house, showing sympathy and consideration for him and, above all, giving him hope for the future! If this is not done, a man, who is capable of anything, becomes a beast in no time at all, and if you want him

to be a beast and not a human being, it's no use asking him to behave like a human being.[3]

Man, who is capable of anything! One must see this fearful formula both ways: he creates and inherits the twentieth century and cries out against it; he will, in Faulkner's terms, "prevail" against it.

The mother in *Two Women* blurts out her explanation of war and crime. She inverts causes and oversimpli-
fies, but Moravia thus, very shrewdly, forces the reader
to think through man's decline through war.

> "Everything's changed?—rubbish!" I cried. "It's you
> who were simply waiting for a war—you and your sons
> and that crook Clorindo and those Moroccan mur-
> derers and the whole lot of you—so that you could
> let yourselves go and do all the things you would never
> have dared to do in normal times. Rubbish! And I tell
> you, all this won't last so very long, and one of these
> days everything will come right again and then you
> and your sons and Clorindo will find yourselves in
> trouble, in bad trouble, and you'll discover that morals
> and religion and law still exist and that honest people
> count for more than crooks." At these words Vin-
> cenzo, half dotty as he was—he who had stolen all his
> landlord's belongings—shook his head and said:
> "Golden words, golden words indeed!" But Concetta
> merely shrugged her shoulders and said: "What are
> you getting so excited about? Live and let live, that's
> what I say." Rosario laughed outright and said: "You,
> Cesira, you're a pre-war woman, and all of *us*—my
> brother and I, Rosetta, my mother and Clorindo—*we*
> all belong to *after* the war. Now look at me, for in-
> stance, I went to Naples with a load of American food
> and Army sweaters, sold it at once, made up a load of
> stuff to sell in Ciociaria—and here's the result," and
> he took out a bundle of bank notes and waved them

under my nose. "I made more in one day than my father has in the last five years. Everything's changed, the old days are gone, and you've got to get used to the idea. And why do you get so worked up about Rosetta? She's realized, too, that there was one way of thinking before the war and a different way now, and she's cottoned on to it and learned how to live.[4]

Moravia is seeing ahead. The mother is wrong; the old days will not tie people down; a new ethic will be needed. This can mean nothing but an ethic of the modern city (state), an existential ethic emerging from Camus's "moment of supreme tension."

Again, in *Two Women*, mother and daughter strike out through the doomsday countryside. There is a memorable reflection, peculiarly feminine and creative, of the war and the earth. They, the war and the earth, are the opposites, not the country and the city.

We walked for some distance. The road was deserted and even in the fields there was not a living soul to be seen. To a town person who did not understand such things, it might have looked like a normal countryside; but I who had been a peasant before I had been a city dweller could see that it was a countryside abandoned. You could see signs of this everywhere: the clusters of grapes in the vineyards ought to have been harvested, instead they were still hanging among leaves that were yellowed, over-golden, some even brown and withered, the grapes half eaten by wasps and lizards. The maize, in some places, was lying flat and in disorder and full of weeds, and the ears were ripe, almost red. All around the fig trees there lay quantities of figs which had fallen from the branches through being too soft, and were now broken and burst open and pecked by birds. There was not a peasant to be seen and I supposed they must all have run away. And yet it was a beautiful day, warm and serene, a real country day. That is what war is like, I said to myself: everything looks normal and yet, underneath, war penetrates like a boring worm in wood and people get frightened and run away, while the countryside, for its part, continues with complete indifference to throw off fruit and corn and grass and trees as though nothing were happening.[5]

There is a breathless restraint here and a palpable diction. The woman's thinking is more deeply inflected and characterized than is usually the case in Moravia's work. The images of earth and woman begin to merge very subtly in anticipation of the sexual storm to come. The uncanny and the mundane are grasped with extraordinary balance.

In this century history and the state are functions of the city and media-man. The nineteenth century ends with World War II. Moravia is clearly one of those responsible, in letters, for the birth of the image of the twentieth century. There is a touch of melancholy, rather than nostalgia, as Moravia, at the height of his maturity, puts the "news" in the voices of the women. Men have had their say.

When the noise had completely died away, I left the field and went to look; and I saw that there were several small holes in the suitcase and that there were a few brass shell cases, as long as my little finger, on the road. There was no doubt about it, then: the plane had been aiming at *us*, for there was no one else on the road. "Curse and blast them," I said to myself, and I was filled with an intense hatred for the war: that airman did not know us, he was, I daresay, a nice young man of Rosetta's age and merely because there was a war going on he had tried to kill us, just for an idle whim, so to speak, like a sportsman out walking in the woods with his dog who shoots haphazard into a tree and says to himself: "I'll kill something, even if it's only a sparrow." Indeed we were just a couple of sparrows, we two, shot at in an idle moment by a sportsman who, if the sparrows fall dead, leaves them where they are since they're of no use to him. "Mum," said Rosetta after a little, as we walked along, "you said in the country there wasn't any war, and yet that man tried to kill us." "My dear child," I answered, "I was wrong. The war is everywhere, in the country just as much as in the town." [6]

This, then, is the context in which to study crime and nihilism in microcosm.

Though events in *The Conformist* center around violence, crime, perversion, and murder, this book is essentially a devastating picture of moral nihilism. Moravia writes a terrible indictment of the stifling and perverting effects of fascism on the human soul. Marcello Clerici, a young Fascist official, is terrified at the thought of being strange and different or unlike everyone else. In his struggle for conformity he will resort to any means, however sinister or evil. Marcello is aware of his "abnormality" and "unnaturalness" at a very early age. He relates his childish pleasure in cutting down flowers and later in the killing of lizards.

The transition from flowers and plants to living creatures was imperceptible, as it is in nature. Marcello could not have said when it was that he discovered that the same pleasure he derived from smashing plants and cutting the heads off flowers could be found, even more intensely and profoundly, by inflicting the same kind of violence on living creatures. It may have been mere chance that encouraged him along this road . . . or it may have been incipient boredom and satiety that put into his head the idea of searching for new material on which to exercise his still unconscious cruelty. However . . . one quiet afternoon when everyone in the house was asleep, Marcello found himself . . . face to face with a slaughtered mass of lizards. There were five or six of them he had managed to hunt out, by various methods . . . striking them down with a single blow of his cane just at the moment when . . . they sought to flee for shelter. . . . He was standing in front of the cement footpath where the lizards lay, his cane grasped firmly in his fist . . . the excitement that had filled him during the slaughter—no longer pleasantly glowing, as it had been then, but already becoming tainted with remorse and shame. He was aware, too, that on this occasion there was not only the usual feeling of cruelty and power but an additional, special agitation that was new to him and inexplicably physical; and . . . he had a vague feeling of alarm. He felt as though he had discovered within himself a characteristic that was completely abnormal . . . that he ought to be ashamed of, that he must keep secret . . . because it might result in cutting him off forever from the society of those his own age.[7]

This passage has an ominous ring. Moravia seems to be setting the scene for the development of Marcello's cruelty (he speaks of his "still unconscious cruelty") which will be directed against "living creatures"—his fellow man. Marcello's terror of abnormality reaches a climax in an adolescent incident in which he believes he has killed a man. The man, a former priest, has made homosexual advances toward Marcello. Too young and inexperienced to detect the exact nature of Lino's friendship, Marcello is only vaguely repulsed by the man. Lino promises Marcello a revolver in a vain effort to gain certain favors. At their last meeting, Marcello, believing that

Lino has tricked him and gone back on his promise, flies
into a rage and shoots the man.

> Later, thinking over what had happened, Marcello
> could not help recalling that the mere touch of the
> cold butt of the weapon had aroused in his mind a
> temptation of the most ruthless and bloodthirsty
> kind; but at that moment all he was aware of was a
> violent pain in his head where he had knocked it
> against the wall, and an acute sense of irritation and
> repugnance toward Lino. The latter had remained on
> his knees beside the bed; but when he saw Marcello
> take a step backward and point the revolver at him
> . . . he cried dramatically, "Shoot, Marcello . . .
> kill me . . . yes, kill me like a dog." It seemed to
> Marcello that he had never hated him so much as at
> that moment, for that repulsive mixture of sensuality
> and austerity, of repentance and lust; and in a manner
> that was both terrified and deliberate—just as though
> he felt he had to comply with the man's request—he
> pressed the trigger.[8]

As Marcello leaves the house unobserved, Moravia again
gives us an ominous forewarning. "As he walked there
was reflected in his consciousness, as in a mirror, the
picture of himself, a boy in shorts with some books under his arm, walking down the cypress-bordered drive, an
incomprehensible figure full of gloomy foreboding."[9]

Burdened with guilt and fear over his abnormal nature, Marcello seeks absolution by living in complete
conformity with other men. His whole life becomes a
desperate attempt to negate any thoughts or feelings
which may be exclusively his and which may differ from
the thoughts or feelings of others. Curiously, his fiancé
observes, "Most people want to be different from everyone else . . . but you're just the opposite; anyone would
think you wanted to be like everyone else."[10] Marcello's

passion to be "like everyone else" forces his acceptance
of the Fascist dictatorship and his willingness to go along
with the power structure at all costs. As a Fascist official
he is drawn into a role of a political spy. Ironically, Marcello's obsessive struggle to "belong" through conscious
conformity leads him to estrangement and alienation
from himself. Too late, he realizes the tragedy of a life
inauthentically lived.

It is important to remember that evil and sadism and
fascism do not appear before our eyes nor are they de-
terministic continuations of each other at different orders of abstraction. There is here, as with Sartre, a social
criticism. Society is the garden that produces and re-
claims the sticky blood of its transactions. The alienation of Marcello is a powerful incentive for him to attempt to deny his superfluousness by committing crimes
actively in the garden and later, passively in the street
for Mussolini. Children's lives are disfigured and tor-
tured in this bourgeois garden, and the offer of love,
homosexual or otherwise, inspires these stunted beings to
reach for their guns. Behind the male protest hides a
moral dwarf.

The humanism of the Enlightenment has become a
sham because it nurtures ideals that must come to grief
in the garden (to change the figure and use the garden
as the body with its vegetative imperatives). Bad faith is
forced on the child—he is a victim. He perpetuates and
repeats bad faith—he is an agent. He has torn the lizards
apart; he has experienced blood on his hands; he is nauseated by the swollenness of his vegetative being; his in-
timations of Being are converted into guilt. It is bad luck
that his past and future will haunt him with social
echoes of this traumatic encounter, but Moravia would
never use this as the stuff of a novel if it had all been
fated by some inexorable modern oracle. No, the suffering boy, his unfaithful mother, Mussolini himself, they

are all free! Freedom is to existentialism what fate was to classicism: a metaphor. Oedipus pretends to be destined and the modern protagonist pretends to be free. But the style of Oedipus is persistent ("free"), while our modern hero still receives his nervous system from the vegetation and his methods from his mother ("fate"). So, "evil" is a priori coeval with the nervous system, yet it is ineluctable with ontology. One more of the existential paradoxes that Moravia moves through his work so naturally.

In "Mother's Boy," a story from *More Roman Tales*, Moravia details the most insidious kind of nihilism— nihilism which is programmed, which is passed through the generations, from a mother to her son. Gigi, poor and unemployed, resorts to stealing articles from automobiles by means of a flat tire trick. He tells of the first incident after he has stolen a camera and tried to conceal it at home. His mother quickly discovers what he has done.

> She . . . like a real mother, merely said to me, in a quiet voice: "It's no good you're hiding things, give them to me. A hiding-place can always give you away, your mother never will. . . . Your mother loves you, nobody can love you as your mother does." I was upset, I confess; and not so much because of the camera as because of the reproof which I felt in her words: how could I have thought that my mother would not understand and forgive me? This, then, was the beginning; and thenceforth, whenever I played this trick, I took the things to her; and she, as well as hiding them for me, also undertook the selling of them, for she was very smart and was acquainted with a great many people and knew the value of things better than the employees at the pawnshop.[11]

Even though Gigi evidences relief as his mother accepts his criminal involvement, we cannot help but feel that unconsciously Gigi has brought the camera home for the purpose of parental reproof over an act which he knows is wrong. His mother professes to love him, but this love is superficial, for it is uncritical, object-oriented. The mother fails her son; she not only excuses his criminal actions but becomes a part of those very actions by undertaking to sell the stolen items as well. Indeed, she not only condones, she also encourages evil by her own participation. It is interesting that Camus in *Malentendu* should have hit upon the same metaphor of a mother and child in symbiotic underworldliness, in a criminal conspiracy together. This perversion of the *Pietá* is particularly frightening and taboo, as frightening, perhaps, as incest, if not simply another version of that highest of literary crimes. Could the reason be that a private, illegal, *intimate* relationship is a chilling reminder of that contingent luck on which law and all institutions depend? These gaps in conscience, these superego lacunae exist, we say, but not in normal relationships, not in the same field as the finer, saving instincts. But a mother's love for her child? What could be more normative and so, more shocking? A mother, her child, and crime: this is the very essence of the banality of evil, the genotype of nihilism with which we are all infected and against which, according to Moravia's lights, we must rebel.

In another description of the mother-son relationship, Gigi says:

But above all a mother, because of the love she bears her son, will take his side against the whole world, even though, as in my case, he is a thief; for she is the only person who understands him and knows why he has committed a theft; and who, knowing it, helps him to remain free and unrepentant. All this, and a good deal more, I would feel at the moment when I arrived home in the evening after chasing cars all day long. . . . I used to hand over the stuff to her and she

would go at once and shut it up in her chest-of-draw-
ers, and I would go into the kitchen and she would
put my bowl on the table in front of me, and I would
eat and she would watch me. We scarcely spoke; like
animals we understood each other by a glance.[12]

This last sentence shows how subtly Moravia can reveal
the animallike quality of nihilism—its unhumanness. The
mother and son no longer need to communicate in verbal, human ways, but "like animals" they understand
each other "at a glance." The love expressed here is an
animal love, predicated on crime. In every case "animal"
must be interpreted contextually. Here it is an epithet,
but elsewhere it is a sign of biological solidarity.

Gigi feels that his mother understands him, knows
why he must steal, and therefore helps him to remain
free and unrepentant. The author presents this as a
masterly and ironic insight. Gigi is "free," yes, but only
from the law and only for the time being. He is certainly not free in the existential meaning of freedom; he
is not free to choose. His mother has become the goddess or priestess who accepts all offerings, all gifts. In return she gives total sustenance (forgiveness, absolution).
But the price Gigi pays for this absolution is his freedom.

Gigi begins seeing a neighborhood girl who works in
her parent's drapery shop. They are attracted to each
other and Gigi is surprised to find a woman who
"showed me the same affection that I had so far imagined only my mother could have for me." [13] Gesuina
senses Gigi's criminal involvements but still loves him.
However, her love is critical for she is able to ask, "Don't
you see, Gigi, that what you're doing is wrong?" [14]
Though Gigi denies that he is doing anything wrong, he
begins to examine the different attitudes of the two
women. He tells his mother about Gesuina; that the girl
loves him and wants him to join her in the shop, even
though she knows of his behavior and condemns it. Dis-

tressed, the mother tells Gigi that all he does is right and if he is happy she will also be content. Here it is obvious that Gigi has wished for his mother's disapproval all along. "But now, for some reason, I wanted her to say to me, as Gesuina did: 'What you are doing is wrong, you must change your manner of life and settle down'; but I knew that this would be asking too much of her; it would have been like making her admit that she had not been a good mother because she had encouraged me instead of condemning me. And so the evening, like all our evenings, ended in silence." [15]

Once engaged, Gigi finds himself behind the counter of the draper's shop. But he soon begins to weaken and cannot convince himself that it is better to be selling ribbon and thread than creating flat tires on parked cars. In an ironic, absurd twist of events, Gigi is finally confronted with the reality of his crimes. Noticing a car with a flat tire, his first reaction is one of sympathy and he feels an impulse to warn the owner. "But at the same moment I looked inside the car, saw a handsome, solid leather bag on the seat and caught myself thinking: 'I'll pinch it and take it to my mother and I'm damned if I'll go back to Gesuina, and my mother's the only person who can understand me and I'll start life with my mother again.' " [16] Absorbed in these thoughts, Gigi fails to notice a man's approach. The man angrily accuses him of purposely causing the flat tire in order to steal the leather bag. Gigi denies the accusation but the man "seized hold of me by the collar and hissed between his teeth . . . 'You can thank heaven I'm not a nasty kind of chap. Now change that wheel if you don't want me to call a policeman.' Well, I had to give in . . . after all those other flat tires, I had to put on a good wheel in place of a tyre which I had *not* punctured. I dirtied my hands and my clothes. . . . When I had finished, he got into the car and said: 'That's fine; but next time you'll go and change the wheel at the Regina Coeli prison.' " [17]

This incident of tire-changing brings the full impact of Gigi's crimes into dreadful focus. Until now his crimes have only been abstractions. This event forces reality or knowledgeability upon him. Crime can no longer be tolerated; he must change his life. His crimes have been grasped by a conscience; grasped just enough to be meaningful. But for Morvia's characters, a seemingly small insight has the profoundest potential for life change.

The overdetermined logic of dreams is at work here. The flattened tire is a clear castration symbol. Gigi deflates the vehicle of the powerful, wealthy man; he steals a valuable: patricide and incest. At the same time, on the ethical level, the flattened tire is the sign of nothingness, nihilism, of Gigi's empty life. The "false" accusation at the end of the story-dream is the deflected evening of the score at both levels, the psychological and the ethical. This is the shift toward authenticity: Where id was there shall ego be, or, in existential terms: where It was there shall I be!

In "Rain in May," a young man takes a waiter's job in a small restaurant outside Rome and falls in love with the proprietor's daughter. The couple plan to rid themselves of the girl's mean, evil-tempered, tyrannical father.

> And so Dirce and I came to an understanding and together we determined upon the means and the day and the hour. Tocchi, in the morning, used to go down into the cellar to fetch up the wine for the day, together with Dirce carrying the big bottle to be filled. . . . We decided that I should join them down in the cellar and, while Tocchi bent down to tap the wine-cask, I should hit him over the head with a short iron bolt that was used for poking the fire. Then we would pull away the steps and would say he had fallen down and broken his skull.[18]

At that crucial moment when the young man is ready to enter the cellar, Moravia brings about a reversal of events. The writing is terrifying, magnificent and might easily be straight out of Dostoyevsky himself.

At that moment the door leading into the garden was opened and a man with a wet sack over his shoulders came in—a carter. Without looking at me, he said: "Give us a hand, mate, will you?"—and I, automatically, still holding the poker, followed him out. . . . his cart, loaded with stones, had stuck in the mud as it went in at the gate and the horse was unable to move it. The carter, an ugly, deformed, bestial-looking man, appeared beside himself with rage. I . . . placed two stones under the wheels and pushed. . . . it was raining torrents on the thick, green hedges of elder and the acacias in flower, which smelt strongly; the cart did not move and the carter swore. He took up his whip and laid on to the horse with the handle; then, becoming ferocious, he seized hold of the poker which I had placed on top of the gate-post. You could see that he was beside himself with rage not because of the cart but because of his whole life, and that he hated the horse like a person. "He's going to kill it now," I thought; and I was just going to shout: "No, leave that poker alone." But then I thought that, if he killed the horse, I was safe. It seemed to me that the whole of my fury was passing into the body of that carter, who appeared like a man possessed; and he did, in fact, hurl himself on the shafts of the cart, give another push, and then start laying on to the horse's head with the poker. At the first blow I shut my eyes, and then I heard him continuing to strike, and all the time my strength was failing and I was almost fainting; and then I opened my eyes again and saw that the horse had fallen on its knees and that he was still hit-

ting it—not, now, to make it get up but actually to
kill it. The horse fell down on its side, kicked its feet
in the air, in a feeble way; and then dropped its head
in the mud. The carter, panting for breath, his face
distorted, threw away the poker and gave the horse a
shove—but without conviction: he knew he had killed
it. I passed close by him, but without brushing against
him, and started walking along the main road. The
tram came past on its way in to Rome and I ran and
jumped on it and then looked back and saw, for the
last time, the inn sign: "Osteria dei Cacciatori, Proprietor Antolio Tocchi", amongst the rain-soaked
May foliage.[19]

From sexuality to crime, the Moravian gyroscope
swings back and forth in a millenarian rhythm. Dostoyevsky and Tolstoy lay the blows of our age on defense-
less old horses in a great existential image of evil. One
day while walking, Nietzsche throws himself on the neck
of an actual old horse to intercept the driver's blows, and
the last phase of his madness is begun. Moravia's use of
this received ensign—of crime from the philosophical
angle of refraction—is instructive. Roskolnikov and Por-
fieri Petrovitch discuss the murder of the old louse of a
landlady from a point of view revealingly adolescent in
its philosophy. Moravia is more centrifugal, like Sartre
he is cool, taking an overview.

"Crime at the Tennis Club" might almost have been
inspired by one of the themes from *Being and Nothingness*: sadism (a critical variety of nothingness) as a *donnée*. The sadist forces the prostitute to parade nakedly,
absurdly about. He remains dressed, pretending to exist
at her expense. Now, Moravia is very close to this in his
story, though Sartre's book had not been written when
the young Italian had begun to see crime in a new way.

Then—whether it was that she became ashamed of
displaying her already middle-aged body, or that a

flash of consciousness, penetrating the fumes of wine
showed her to herself as she actually was, flushed and
dishevelled, her breast half bared, surrounded by bru-
talized men in that little white room . . . the sport
had excited the five men. Two held her by the arms,
while the other three pulled her dress right down to
her waist exposing a torso yellowish and puckered,
with flabby, sallow breasts.[20]

Later they will kill her with a blow from a bottle.
Here is the image behind the icon, the poor mare that
has been beaten steadily for over eleven decades in and
out of literature. The boys, after playing "Fathers and
Sons," begin their program of sadism. In existential
terms, the existence of the Other is made contingent, a
servomechanism of the narcotized torturer. Why? What
lies behind this sadomasochistic encounter (for the
"princess" is almost an obligatory victim) in philosophical rather than pyschological reasoning? What, in short,
after this polymorphous scenario has been rehearsed for
over a century, is the cause beneath the cause? The reason beneath the psychological reason is that each person
attempts to use the other in order to realize, to prove his
own Being. The overcrowding or failure of sadism leads
to authentic need and need's failure is the announcement of sadism. A humble, simple formula for a generation for whom love is *de trop* and for whom the brief
affair with history, begun by Napoleon, has turned out
to be an obscene experiment.

The "Chinese Vase," like "Rain in May," presents a
tale of life change through crime. A hopeless young man
in desperate circumstances is reduced to selling old junk
and bottles. Moravia gives us a poignant picture of the
man's despair.

As long as there's life there's hope, so they say; but I,
during that horrible black winter of rain and misery,

had let myself go all to pieces, partly from tiredness and partly from the job I was doing . . . I had no hope left. . . . owing to my neglect of myself I could be considered, by this time, to be really ugly. I shaved and had my hair cut perhaps once a month, perhaps not, so that I looked like a savage; I wore an overcoat that was green with age and all darns and patches . . . frayed trousers, and cheap shoes that had lost all colour and shape. . . . I frightened people, in fact; but I enjoyed frightening them because I had become degraded and I wanted to reach the lowest depths of degradation. And meanwhile the winter seemed to go on for ever, and the sky never cleared and it never stopped raining, and I seemed to be dragging myself, with all my rags and hand-barrow, along a tunnel with no openings and no light, somewhere under the ground.[21]

Surely this picture of despair is more than just a well-phrased fictional description. When we recall Moravia's hideous exile in the mountains during the winter of 1945, we sense that the desolation in this story stems from a very real experience.

In spite of his degradation, the young man manages to acquire a girl friend. Marietta is a servant to an elderly man who collects rare and antique vases. Though at first violently opposed, Marietta is finally persuaded to help her boy friend steal a valuable Chinese vase. She believes that the money obtained from the vase will help them to get married. The man can find no real answer as to why he must steal the vase.

But during the following days I started insisting again that we ought to take the vase. I don't know why I was so set on it: at the bottom of my heart I didn't really want to marry Marietta. Perhaps it was because I had become so degraded and, as I have already said,

I wanted to reach the lowest depths of degradation; perhaps it was because I took pleasure in being cruel to Marietta; perhaps there was some other reason that I myself didn't know. Anyhow, I tormented her, telling her that if she didn't steal the vase it was a sign that she didn't love me; and I went on about it so much that in the end she made up her mind to it.[22]

After the theft is accomplished, the jangled young man, suddenly realizing that he is a thief and has now sunk to the lowest depths, tries to get hold of himself. He escapes to an eating house to "get some food to restore my strength and help me sort out my ideas." [23] The handcart is left outside and through the trickery of a group of small boys the valuable Chinese vase is destroyed. But Moravia uses this senseless sequence of events to symbolize his protagonist's despair and subsequent life renewal or life change.

I realized however, almost at once, that it was not only the vase that had gone but also that whole period of my life during which I had been a bottle-man and had loved Marietta and had stolen the vase. I left the handcart where it was . . . and I went off to see my friend Gesualdo, who lived not far off, in Villa della Pace. When he saw me looking so upset, he asked me what had happened. "Nothing, nothing," I answered; "all I need is a wash-tub of hot water and a piece of soap and a razor. And then, if you really want to make me a present, find me a pair of trousers, a clean shirt and a tie . . . I'll repay everything as soon as I can."

When I left Gesualdo's house I was a different person; and this different person was now filled with hope instead of despair; and instead of going back to the place where I had so far lived, I went off to the other side of the town and found a lodging there with a family of my acquaintance. A few days later the weather was fine, and I, in a waiter's white jacket, clean and well shaved, fresh and brisk, was serving customers in the garden of the Osteria di Malagrotta, twenty kilometers out of Rome. Marietta I have never seen again; but I don't want to be harshly judged on that account. It was not treacherousness, nor wickedness, nor cowardice. It was simply like turning the page of a book and discovering that the chapter is finished.[24]

Gide's term is losing currency in existential literature. There are no "gratuitous crimes"; they are equally meaningful or else equally absurd.

Why does Moravia continually utilize crime to point out man's absurd condition? Moravia's characters must often recognize the absurdity of life through crime before they can experience the need to affirm life. Confronted with the criminal act, man is forced to choose: to continue to wallow in the death throes of nihilism or to commit himself to life. In recognizing the extreme of human degradation through crime and violence, these characters seem to sense the other extreme, that of compassion and love—the highest self at the other end of the pole. Moravia uses crime to symbolize the conflict between nihilism and death on one hand, and affirmation of life on the other. As the absurdity of degradation and crime is revealed, man is compelled to choose. He must choose to continue in violence or go beyond the absurdity of violence; to discard the absurd and fashion something from nihilism, from the nothing.

As we study Moravia's men and women, we become aware of the dualism inherent in their characters. An astute critic, Charles Glicksberg, acknowledges, "The singular paradox of modern literature is that in portraying characters in terms of the negative, it must still endow them with a central self that passes judgment. . . .

The mind that passes judgment on the meaninglessness of the universe assumes that it can recognize meaning and therefore represents an instrument capable of resisting and perhaps of overcoming the blind bludgeoning of the will." [25] Although applied to contemporary literature in general, this statement is astonishingly accurate in describing Moravia's characters. Hence we have the "fall" (crime, violence) and the "recoil of conscience" [26] (the recognition of options).

Merciless in his demand for truth and self-honesty, Moravia concedes that the self can only manage to affirm life after it confronts the painful truth of nothingness. Here the existential correlatives, rebellion and conversion, are linked hand in hand. As the self or conscience rebels against the absurdity of nothingness, the possibility for conversion becomes explicit. This is the paradox then: crime becomes the essential act by which the existential protagonist struggles to transform the negative into the positive. The absurd is transformed into a more thoughtful, sympathetic doctrine of man's nature. Existentially, then, this becomes a cry for commitment, and the paradox is completed. Moravia's characters through crime and the recognition of crime as nihilism, absurdity, and death, can, with the same consciousness with which they perceived the nothingness, also reject it or recoil from it. They are aware of the choice between remaining "nothing" and refuting the nothingness of existence. Moravia's people more often choose the existential role of commitment, of changing their lives. In direct confrontation with his own violence, and the recognition of that violence as insane, nihilistic, absurd, man is forced into seeing an opposite possibility —commitment to a higher rationality. Revelation manifests itself through crime. Crime, for Moravia, acts as a powerful agent to change man's life. Crime can vitiate further crime.

7

Self-Delusion or Bad Faith

Self-delusion for Moravia is no more than giving in to the forces of narcissism, the nostalgia of the flesh. Narcissism blinds and deludes man; it proscribes his actions and thinking along paths of falseness (memory) and pretentiousness. Bad faith, then, completes the equation of solipsism and self-delusion. In Moravia, the giving up of the polymorphous past and the accompanying change in thought and action from bad to good faith, is often accomplished with great irony.

In *Conjugal Love*, Moravia gives us a character who is capable of battling his way out of the abyss of self-delusion or narcissism. The plot is old-fashioned and timeworn; a man neglects his wife and her subsequent act of infidelity almost destroys the marriage. Moravia's genius weaves this material into a masterful love story.

Silvio Baldeschi, young, wealthy, well educated, and married to the beautiful Leda, should be a supremely happy man. Instead, he is tormented by a gnawing dissatisfaction and restlessness. He is convinced that only two things can save him—"the love of a woman and artistic creation." [1] His first goal is realized in a completely happy marriage. Inspired by love and convinced that he can become a great writer, Silvio begins the task of writing a novel. However, the work does not progress well. Obsessed with the idea that he has "exhausted all [his] aggressive force in [his] wife's embrace," [2] he persuades Leda that they should sleep apart until he finishes his book. It is clear that falseness and deception have instigated this decision, for Silvio admits retrospectively, "My obsession was still strong and it made me forget how much selfishness, and therefore falseness, had been at the root of it." [3] Here is extraordinary hindsight and insight: "selfishness and therefore falseness."

In a stroke reminiscent of Mann and foreshadowing the scandal of *Ghost at Noon*, the author, with great psychological deftness, lays the predicate for the sexual summation of this extraordinary novel of creativity, the artist, love, and bad faith. Early in the story we learn that Silvio has hired a barber to come to the villa every morning to shave him. Moravia proceeds with warm, sensuous images to reveal Silvio's unconscious matchmaking between Leda and Antonio. This is confirmed as Silvio refuses to dismiss Antonio despite his wife's bitter complaints concerning the barber's advances. Later the barber's body, pressed against Silvio's arm and shoulder, produces a "frantic repugnance" in the deluded author.

All this is no clinical or reductive case history; it is, instead, an allegory. The polymorphous sexuality and the poorly sublimated, compulsive novel-writing of Silvio represent a split in the existential libido. The sexuality is a metaphor for the vicissitudes of "creativity" and *impotenza* and the artist. Just as Freud revealed how the everyday contacts of life may stand for the erotic agenda, so authors like Faulkner (in *Sanctuary*) and Moravia show the reverse: sexuality is simply a sign, at the lowest order of abstraction, of the existential everyday, the "terrible power of the quotidian."

At length, Silvio finishes the novel. The fulfillment of his two goals in life now seems a reality. In a state of joyous exultation, Silvio sets out for the local village to secure paper for the final copying of his manuscript.

Moravia's favorite device of utilizing nature to let us feel a character's mood is beautifully executed.

> The trap started off down the drive, where the first rays of the morning sun were already playing, skirted the old boundary wall and turned into the main road. The air was mild, and the soft splendor of autumn lay upon all things; I looked round over the countryside, already partly despoiled and weary looking, and all about me, in that accurate light, so different from the devouring glare of summer, all things were clearly visible, each thing could be clearly distinguished, even to the finest detail and the subtlest shade of color; and I could not have enough of looking. . . . There were patches of verdigris, of a poisonous blue, upon the white walls of farm buildings; there was moss, yellow as gold, on the weathered rooftiles of a little church that looked like a barn; there were big, pale green acorns among the darker leaves of a young oak that hung out over the road from the field beside it. I rejoiced in these and other similar minute details as though they had been rich with some ineffable meaning; and I was aware that I owed this new way of looking at things, as though I were in love with them, to my own happiness, which, also, was new and ineffable.[4]

As we read this masterly mood study, we are again aware of the author's thesis that love brings about a conversion, a radical change in the way of seeing and feeling, a "new way of looking at things."

Silvio begins the final typing of his manuscript, but is assailed by a feeling of remoteness and absurdity—"I simply could not get the sense of the words that I had written with such ardor a few days before . . . it seemed to me that they had no weight, no meaning."[5] In a desperate attempt to be objective about his work, Silvio

begins to jot down his observations and ends with the
following conclusions:

> *The book does not count.* . . . the book was written
> in a state of mind of the most perfect and enthusiastic
> happiness and that is certainly the best that can be
> expected from the author. Indeed the latter, while he
> was writing it, was convinced that he had created a
> masterpiece. It follows from this that the author ex-
> pressed himself in the book as he really is—a man
> lacking in creative feeling, a mere daydreamer, well-
> intentioned, sterile. This book is the faithful mirror
> of such a man.[6]

This painful self-assessment leads Silvio to seek the
comfort of his wife's embrace. Unable to find Leda in
her room and thinking she has gone for a moonlight
stroll, Silvio leaves the villa in search of her.

> The white gleam of the moonlight on the gravel
> reminded me of our walk the night before to the farm
> buildings; and suddenly, in my state of combined
> despair and exultation, I was overcome with the de-
> sire to do, now, that thing which it had not been
> possible for me to do then. I would make love to
> Leda on the threshing floor, by the light of that
> magnificent full moon, in the silence of the sleeping
> countryside, with all the passion that came to me
> from the sense of my own impotence. It was cer-
> tainly a very natural, very logical, very ordinary im-
> pulse that suggested this plan to me; but this time I
> was content to let myself go, both in feeling and
> action, like a peasant who seeks, in the docile embrace
> of his wife, comfort and a sort of compensation for
> damage done by a hailstorm. After all, nothing re-
> mained to me, in the wreck of my ambition, but to
> accept my status as a human being, similar in all

respects to that of other men. After that night I would be content to be just a decent fellow with some knowledge of letters and modestly conscious of his own limitations, but at the same time the lover, and the beloved, of a young and beautiful wife.[7]

It is then that Silvio discovers his wife in a shocking act of infidelity with the village barber. Clearly, Silvio seems to have engineered this illicit relationship between Leda and Antonio. Unconsciously he has assigned to the barber those acts which he himself has felt incapable of performing. Moravia also gives us an insight into Silvio's feeling of attraction for the barber. This unconscious homosexuality is one more ironic aspect of Silvio's narcissism.

Shaken by his wife's infidelity, Silvio is nevertheless capable of understanding how his own conduct has precipitated this act.

I was overwhelmed by what I had witnessed, but I made a great effort to control myself and to take a detached view of it. . . . There flashed upon me, however, a sudden suspicion that this effort to be objective was merely a device on the part of wounded pride; and I said to myself that I could reason and understand as much as I liked, but the fact remained: I had been cruelly deceived, my wife had betrayed me with a barber, and this betrayal stood between me and my wife. At this thought I felt a sharp pain; and I realized that, for the first time since I had seen Leda in Antonio's arms, I was assuming the role that had been forced upon me—that of the husband of an unfaithful wife. But at the same time I knew that I was neither willing nor able to accept that position. I had not hitherto been a husband like other husbands; our relations had been just as I had wished them to be and not as our married state might have prescribed; and so they must remain. I must continue to be reasonable and, above all, understanding. This was my vocation, and not even betrayal could justify my abandoning it. . . . I recognized . . . in [Leda's] actions the furious but short-lived impetus of the involuntary infraction of an acknowledged rule. . . . Her intrigue with the barber—which, in all probability, would not survive that night—and her ties with me, of a year's duration, were two different things, on two entirely different planes. . . . But this thought, far from comforting me as it should have done, depressed me even more. It was one more proof of my incapacity, of my feebleness, my impotence. To me, both creative art and my wife were granted only through pity, through affection, benevolence, reasoned goodwill; the fruits of this concession would never be either love or poetry, but merely a process of forced, decorous composition, a tepid, chaste felicity. Not for me the true masterpiece, not for me the dance on the threshing floor. I was relegated, forever, to mediocrity.[8]

The lucidity of the inner monologues, the device of the author as protagonist, the leashed-in but recrudescent sensuality, the impulses and their failing defenses and final transformations; all these things, together with the most elegant narrative style, reveal Moravia as one of the twentieth-century masters of the novella, with many of the same literary strengths as Thomas Mann.

For instance, in passing, we are stimulated into the old fascinating contradiction between sexuality and creativity. Silvio attempts in the crudest manner to bludgeon his "creative organs" into a program. He attempts to redirect his libido in order to create a work of art; in order to fashion a brainchild. This attempt to commit parthenogenesis brings our hero to grief and humiliation because it is rank *hubris*—"selfishness and therefore false."

Again, the ambivalent relationship with the barber, who will cuckold him, leads one's associations to the collapse of Aschenbach in "Death in Venice." These sensual transactions between barber and client, at once disguised and blatently narcissistic, provide a rich source of insight for those authors who combine psychological perception with exquisite tact.

Anton Chekov is absolutely original in his understanding and plotting of the faithless relationship. Chekov can trace the changes of infidelity as they sometimes become the catalyst for love and loyalty, but Moravia, too, takes a dramatic and different point of view. Though Silvio does not reach the stature of Chekovian responsibility, he does attain to a unique Moravian candor and saving irony.

In existential terms the past is buried in the flesh. It is a carnal revenant laid only by the calls of the present. This titanic struggle between vegetative nostalgia and Being (the In-Itself against the For-Itself) is the underlying agony of romantic love or love's suffering, or their double, the neurosis.

We have already mentioned the importance of Svevo to the development of Moravia. It is curious that Svevo, too, in *As a Man Grows Older*, has written a great novel on the theme of self-delusion. This work and Moravia's *Conjugal Love* provoke comparison. In both novels the antagonists are egotists and both share the delusion that they are destined to become brilliant writers. In Svevo's work Emilio has given up writing though he still considers himself capable of returning to it and producing a great book.

> For many years now . . . he had written nothing at all, not from any mistrust of his own powers, but from

sheer inertia. His novel, printed on bad paper, had turned yellow on the shelves of the bookshops, but Emilio, who at the time of its publication had been spoken of only as a literary star of the future, had by degrees come to be looked upon as a solid literary asset who had some weight in the petty artistic scales of the city. The original estimate had never been revised, it had merely developed with time into something else. He had too clear a perception of the insignificance of his own work ever to boast about the past; but in art as in life he regarded himself as being still in a preparatory stage, secretly considering his genius to be a powerful machine in process of construction but not yet functioning. He lived in a perpetual state of impatient expectation of something which was to be evolved for him by his brain, namely art, and of something which was to come to him from outside—good fortune, success—as if he had not already passed the age when his vitality was at the full.[9]

As Emilio and Silvio are deluded into thinking themselves creative artists, they both present highly interesting studies in sexuality as well. Silvio sacrifices his love and sexuality under the delusion of artistic fulfillment, while Emilio has never been able to experience love at all. At thirty-five he at last desires a woman and thinks himself to be in love. But he does not really want to become emotionally involved; his needs are, indeed, only for a plaything. He tells the woman he is attracted to that he is unable to become serious and they must act with great prudence, for his career and his family responsibilities come first.

And his family? An only sister who made no claim at all on him, either physically or morally. . . . Of the two it was really he who was the egotist. She was like a mother to him in her unselfish devotion, but this did not prevent him from speaking as if his shoulders were weighed down by the burden of another precious life bound to his own, and of acting as if this weight of responsibility obliged him to go cautiously through life, avoiding all its perils, but also renouncing all its pleasures and all hope of earthly felicity. At the age of thirty-five, the desire for pleasures he had never tasted, for love he had never known surged up in his heart, but with a sense of bitterness and frustration at the thought of all he might have enjoyed; and he was conscious at the same time of a great mistrust of himself, and of the weakness of his own character which hitherto he had had occasion rather to suspect than to prove by actual experience.[10]

Emilio's love is false but he deludes himself into thinking that his feelings are genuine. Unlike Silvio, who at last gives up his pretensions and commits himself whole-heartedly to his love, Emilio is unable to muster the courage of a total commitment.

"During the first two years of our married life my relations with my wife were, I can now assert, perfect." [11] Moravia begins his novel *Ghost at Noon* with a master-stroke of irony. This novel (perhaps because the narrator-protagonist is an intellectual and an artist) is, in many ways as successful as the great short stories. A look at the highly polished plot reveals the author's mature control of the longer form, a mastery he is more famous for in his novellas.

On the surface the story concerns Riccardo Molteni, a serious playwright who, after two "perfect" years of marriage, makes a life change in order, as he thinks, to give his wife the material things she would like. He begins to write for the films in order to purchase a new home and other luxuries. At the same time the marriage drifts apart until Emilia, his wife, begins an affair with the film magnate Battista. Molteni is working on a film version of Homer's *Odyssey* when to his horror his psychoanalytically inclined script collaborator succeeds in drawing a devastating parallel between the Odysseus-Penelope myth and the Riccardo-Emilia disaster. Finally, Emilia is killed in Battista's speeding sports car and Riccardo is left to ponder how it all happened.

Such is the tale our narrator tells; but what really happens in this existential recension of the *Odyssey*? Why is Riccardo's new film career coeval with the start of Emilia's contempt for him and the beginning of the end of their relationship? On their first evening together, Riccardo had urged Emilia to ride with the producer whose expensive sports car held room for only one of them—"I said gaily: 'Emilia, you go on with Battista . . . I'll follow in a Taxi.' " [12] Thus the scenario within the scenario is begun. As his marriage begins to disintegrate under the mysterious pressure of Emilia's contempt, Riccardo finds that his scripting duties have become a slavery to him. For, as he thinks to himself, "he will never see his own name on the posters . . . he can never say . . . in this film I expressed myself . . . this film is *me*." [13] No, only the producer, Battista, has *potenza* while Riccardo must live without identity in work as in love. Here, then, is the defeat of the two categories on which any satisfaction depends—*Lieben und Arbeiten*, love and work, in Freud's famous formula. All the while he struggles with his collaborator, Rheingold, over the *Odyssey*, striving with all his power to keep intact the ancient simplicity and mythic purity of the old story, resisting Rheingold's psychology as if it were the plague. Ironically this often seems to be precisely the antipsychological ax the existentialist is grinding.

After Emilia's accidental death, Riccardo wanders back to Capri where, after his abandonment, he had fantasied a loving reunion with his wife. He half fears and half wants her to materialize to his grief-haunted eyes. She does not, and he realizes that the ghost of the wife that had appeared to him once at noon is gone, too. The revenant is laid, transformed and translated, now, into memory. The final passage is instructive.

> The beach was deserted; and as I came out through the masses of fallen rock with my eyes raised towards the smiling, blue expanse of the sea, the thought of the *Odyssey* came back into my mind, and of Ulysses and Penelope, in those great sea spaces, and was fixed for eternity in the shape in which she had been clothed in life. It depended on myself . . . to find her again . . . only in that way would she be delivered from me, would she be set free from my feelings, could she bend down over me like an image of consolation and beauty.[14]

Here, in a striking shift to the second person as a sign of subjectivity, Moravia has Riccardo begin his existential therapy. The old paradox: his body will remember his wife while his mind, exploding with nostalgia and myth, will begin the process of demystification and sanity. Nostalgia standing in an ontological relationship to classical myth (body to memory) has created Riccardo's ghost at noon, but the yearnings of midday must give way to the lengthening shadows of finitude.

Odysseus has forsaken immortality on that isolated island of Circe to return to home and death—to Penelope. In that great moment he had, to quote Camus, to choose "Ithica, the faithful land." [15] So, homecoming, nostalgia, and consolation are inverted to become an arrow of longing for the future, the future in the present. Buber puts this another way, which seems to mirror Moravia's Odyssean struggle between the ghost and the world, when he says, "No set purpose, no greed, and no anticipation intervene between I and Thou. Desire is transformed as it plunges out of its dream into the appearance." [16] Riccardo's true dialogue with his love and himself begins at the end of this disturbing book. He creates a new function of distance, for, says Buber, "the poem is spokenness, spokenness to the Thou, *wherever* this partner might be." [17] Moravia's strategy exactly.

Buber says that the loving man grasps "non-relatively," and Camus meditates on "all the faces we shall never see." Moravia's ghost is of a piece with these ideas. Riccardo is afflicted by the For-itself feeling; he discerns the enigmatic face of the universe in the ghost of his wife. This For-itself is contradicted sharply by the In-itself of the producer Battista. Battista is a propagandist with a lust, not a love, for the Other. Battista robs the Other of his distance and independence. It is this robbery that Riccardo, like Gigi, has done with once and for all. For Riccardo, the memory of Emilia "bleeds" toward him, she is real to him for the first time. Riccardo's confrontation with the ghost is Sartre's *Le Regard*, the look or gaze of relationship. This gaze—like Kazantzakis's Cretan glance, without hope or fear—is always Moravia's vision of literary closure. His creations bleed toward freedom.

But if Moravia is to be interpreted philosophically, it must be quickly said that seldom since Freud has the psychology of myth been so elegantly exploited and with such a smooth, hovering control. In the novel Riccardo violently rejects the hideous reduction of the *Odyssey* to the banality of a neurosis and, as an author, his argument is irrefutable. The creative artist must always expand meaning (in all of this we are, of course, discussing Moravia when Riccardo speaks as artist)—"the world of Homer is a real world. Homer belonged to a civilization which had developed in accordance with, not in antagonism to, nature." [18]

Still, if art is centripetal then life, in the limit situation, is centrifugal. It is here that psychology can draw its fatal repetitions until, overwhelmed by the evidence against it, the I emerges for election and responsibility. The In-Itself becomes the For-Itself. The It gives way to the I, while the conscience builds on the ruins of the infantile over-I. This is by way of saying that in the boundary situation the artificial orders of abstraction, philosophy and psychology, are smashed just as those other false divisions of past, present, and future are inextricably merged in the choice and the chooser. It is here at the edge that the thrust of consolatory nostalgia is reversed and Being interrupts nothingness. An existentialism like the one being argued for Moravia does not, then, deny or defy the psychology of the depths; rather it insists on it as proof that the soul, too—this is a shocking philosophical suggestion—is a thing of finitude! Only when this last paradox is allowed is God truly dead. It is as if Moravia were making the daring leap in this novel in order to demystify the erotic and the supernatural. When the ghost appears we understand completely that it has risen from the flesh of the one who craves for consolation. There are ghosts, Moravia would seem to argue, just as there is a soul but they are hardly extrasensory; no, to see ghosts or feel a stirring in the psyche's depths, one has only to accept biology and history in earnest or, to put it more simply, one has to open one's arms to one's fate; and to say fate is to speak of the human body in all the vicissitudes of its genetic agenda. Moravia seems to take us to the center of this mystery by risking an image, a ghost, totally alien to this century.

The ghost or image of reality is a reminder of Sartre's definition of man as the being who is not what he is and who is what he is not. That is to say that one is often ghostlike in feeling and identity—in between Being and nothingness—so that one cannot say exactly,

with Freud, that Riccardo has repressed his deeper feelings toward Emilia, nor with Sartre that he *chose* to
forget her only to "remember" her as a ghost after her
death. Sartre, thinking to build up the power of the I,
denies the unconscious as such, but Moravia looks back
again and again. The ambivalence of Riccardo toward
his wife's ghost is Sartre's "battle to the death of consciousness." Riccardo's world has been hemorrhaged by
Emilia's death and, to use Sartre again, she "bleeds" in
his direction; the self-for-the-other is rising from the
tragedy. Hazel E. Barnes insists with her fellow existentialist Sartre that the merging of souls (the ghost)
is impossible; wittily she avers *Ego te amo, Tu me
amas.*[19] Reciprocity is always via the objective case.
Moravia, with the Homeric miracle in mind, is always
more ambiguous.

There is an ambience of bad faith surrounding the
unfortunate mother and daughter of *The Wayward
Wife* who indulge themselves in the false pretensions of
society life. Vainglorious hopes goad their passion to
break into high society. The Foresi's are extremely poor
and it is necessary for them to let two or three rooms in
their apartment. Mother and daughter manage to main-
tain a certain air of distinction and quality because of
the girl's relations with a rich and noble family in the
neighborhood with whom every summer Gemma spends
a couple of months at the family's villa. To Gemma this
world is splendid and desirable. The girl's natural in-
clination toward luxury, vanity, and social pretensions
leads her into a world of dreams and unrealities.

> Furthermore, she was encouraged in her course of
> falseness and vainglory by the very person who should
> have restrained and corrected her, her mother. Be-
> neath her mask of humility and shabbiness there was,
> in the widow Foresi, the same kind of senselessness as

in her daughter. The only difference was that certain far-distant experiences had forced her to repress and lay aside—without however renouncing them—the aspirations which her daughter, still inexperienced, displayed openly. . . . There existed in the mother's mind . . . an unreal picture of a world in which beautiful, noble, rich men and women intermingled clamorous passions, lived in abodes of the utmost luxury, capriciously dissipated their inheritances, permitted themselves, in fact, every kind of indulgence, beyond all moral limits and all social obligations. The kind of indulgences . . . that were denied to vulgar persons or to those like herself and her daughter who were persecuted by misfortune; these had to live according to established and quite conventional rules. . . . From these nostalgic desires on the part of her mother, Gemma derived assurance and inspiration for her own ambitions and falsehoods.[20]

A crisis ensues as Gemma, who has plotted to marry a certain wealthy, young man, discovers that the marriage can never materialize. Crushed, Gemma agrees to marry the lodger, a professor of physics, who has fallen in love with her. Vagnuzzi is a brilliant young man with a promising future, but Gemma regards him as a poor, silly creature.

She had, for things of the intellect, a complete and natural contempt which derived, not only from ignorance, but from a particular concept of human values in which she believed passionately and blindly. According to this concept Vagnuzzi, as a professor and a man of modest origins, was on the lowest rung of the social ladder. At the top of it she placed the aristocratic, wealthy, idle young men whom she met during the summer at the villa.[21]

Gemma resigns herself to the marriage for "now she had no hope left, she no longer desired anything, Vagnuzzi was as good as another." [22] Unable to muster any interest in her house or other womanly occupations, Gemma views her married life with a dismal boredom. She soon forms a close friendship with a Romanian woman, Elvira Coceanu. Elvira is one of Moravia's superbly delineated characters. He gives us a vivid and compelling picture of this unscrupulous woman whose greed and cunning opportunism are masked by a sly, honeyed insincerity. It is easy for Elvira to ingratiate herself with Gemma for they both share the "same prejudices and the same preferences." [23] She is quick to maneuver the bored Gemma into an affair with a certain wealthy young man of Rome.

Gemma is attracted to Vittoni and admires his manner. "It was obvious that Vittoni had always lived among well-bred, self-possessed people; this was shown, too, in his contempt for formalities, in the tone of authority in which he spoke." [24] While in town for certain business reasons, Vittoni wants nothing more than to be pleasantly amused; but the sentimental, romantic Gemma attaches a deeper meaning to their relationship.

> Was not this perhaps love, she wondered? Did not love perhaps mean holding hands, being close together, admiring beautiful things together, being silent together? And thus, beneath her vain, artificial longings, there grew up in her again an old-fashioned, provincial sentimentality. . . . By now Gemma was convinced that she had found the delicate soul she had been looking for. Didn't Vittoni listen to her with a serious expression and eyes full of affectionate understanding? Her husband would have either laughed, or have said something stupid, one of those things that

strip away all enchantment. . . . She decided that Vittoni was perfect and was convinced that she loved him.[25]

Mistrustful of intellect, Gemma can only trust her body, her instinct. Once again we encounter the favorite Moravian device of critically juxtaposing intellect and instinct. Moravia is quick to point out that Gemma's trust in her body is founded on extreme self-delusion and ends in an act of bad faith.

> At last Gemma understood what was about to happen. And, suddenly losing all restraint, she thought of nothing but of being frank at all costs . . . it seemed to her that she could give Vittoni no greater proof of her feeling than this: the giving of her body . . . was a very small and quite ordinary thing in comparison with the surrender that shone out in some of her remarks and attitudes. Only, by a mean pre-ordination, every single thing that she was able to say to her lover was secondhand, and, just when she believed herself to be most frank, she was most false. It was a soul borrowed from the cinema and from popular magazines and cheap novels . . . not hers. Thus did despised intelligence avenge itself. And true frankness, the tumult in the blood, the original, profound impulse of experience—all these were resolved into a few worn-out words like the scanty coins jingling together at the bottom of a poor beggar's pocket.[26]

But all too soon Gemma's exaggerated romantic feelings about her lover are dispelled. Vittoni completes his business in town and prepares to leave for Rome. He suggests that they might write to each other, "thinking not to break completely the already tenuous thread of their relationship and thus to keep her in reserve for the moment when the whim might come upon him to take up with her again." [27] But it is Gemma who sees no point in such a correspondence and has the courage to end the affair. Though caught up in an unreal world of false hopes and aspirations, Gemma is able to assess her acts in the painful light of truth. As she is no longer able to deceive herself regarding Vittoni's character, so must she also face the truth of Elvira's friendship. Realizing this friendship is founded on "questionable collusion," Gemma begins to see through Elvira's pretended kindness.

> In the meantime the character of Elvira Coceanu became no less clearly apparent to her than that of Vittoni . . . she became aware of all her defects with a clarity that was actually exaggerated . . . and, marvelling that she had never noticed these defects before, she now experienced . . . an increasing and intolerable feeling of shame . . . Elvira, with her honeyed manner, her insolence and her cool self-possession, now appeared to Gemma as the living, hateful incarnation of deceitfulness. She felt her to be cold-hearted, false, treacherous, capable of every wickedness, a veritable shrew; and she was afraid of her, too. [28]

When Vittoni leaves, Elvira suggests that she be allowed to live with Gemma and her husband. Gemma is horrified of having this woman, whom she now loathes, in her own home. But her rage gives way to fear as Elvira brandishes insidious threats of blackmail. Gemma has had a chance to discern her husband's fine qualities and feels a genuine affection for him. She also knows herself to be pregnant, "and being sure, from a calculation of the number of months, that this baby was her husband's, was very pleased about it." [29] Gemma agrees to Elvira's proposal for she is filled with fear of losing her husband should he find out about the Vittoni affair.

Moravia now leads Gemma through the painful but liberating act of conversion. Not only has her attitude concerning her husband changed, but also her past hopes and aspirations undergo reversal.

> For the first time Gemma discovered that it is not only material things that can be banished or suppressed. There is also an ideal world in which the soul likes to see itself reflected as in a piece of smooth water. And it has no peace unless it sees this world always clear and transparent. She was not conscious of it, but her hatred of Elvira now went beyond the figure of the woman herself and embraced all the errors and aspirations of her own past life. During those sad winter days . . . as a person who suffers from poisoning may, by a violent crisis, be cleansed in a few hours of all the poisons absorbed during several years—the acute irritability of her state of mind had the effect of liberating her not merely from her former admiration for the Rumanian but also from all the other infatuations that had blinded her ever since the years of adolescence. Through confused suffering she was cured of many fevers, and the complete obscurity that oppressed her was the prelude to a new clarity. This, in proportion to her powers and to the kind of mistakes she had made, would be both feeble and limited. Far preferable, however, to the innocent folly of her mother, or the perversity of Elvira.[30]

Elvira's presence brings a confusion and tension to Gemma's life which can no longer be tolerated. Finally, as Vagnuzzi announces that he has obtained a professorship at the University of Rome, Gemma feels that she will at last be freed from Elvira's tyranny. But Vagnuzzi, unaware of the animosity between the two women, invites Elvira to be their guest in Rome. This thought sends Gemma "out of her wits with rage, making her blood boil, all of a sudden, with frenzied violence. It was like a spark on a heap of dry brushwood: there was nothing left inside her but passion, suffering, uncontrolled carnal feeling. Her eyes, wandering crazily over the table, fixed themselves upon the long, sharp knife . . . her hand reached out to this knife and grasped it. . . . Then . . . she rose to her feet with a strange, mechanical suddenness and threw herself, knife raised in her hand, upon Elvira." [31]

Elvira manages to avoid the blow, but no longer to contain herself and writhing with fury and rage, she screams threats and coarse insults at the near fainting Gemma.

> And in this way poor Vagnuzzi . . . came to hear of his misfortune. But all the time Gemma's pallor was increasing; she appeared to be smitten with giddiness and seized hold of the banisters with both hands. Her husband realized it was not the moment of reproofs and explanations, and, without replying to Elvira who was now railing against him too as though possessed by the devil, he compelled his wife—using no violence but with a delicate masterfulness—to go up to her room and lie down on the bed. He feared that Gemma's disorder might not be a mere passing attack but might become aggravated because of her condition. And so, in fact, it happened. After a few minutes she was taken with a high fever and, soon, with rolling eyes and strange words and gestures, she became delirious. [32]

Gemma's illness lasts over a week. Vagnuzzi keeps a constant and devoted vigil at his wife's bedside. During this time he has the leisure to reflect calmly upon the things that have happened. As in *Conjugal Love*, Moravia shows us the cuckolded husband who goes beyond the initial absurd conventional reaction of pained and angry contempt. Moravia, more than any other contemporary writer, realizes that mature and genuine feeling cannot tolerate or be circumscribed by conventional responses. The kind of love or feeling which is truly mature and truly real must allow for differences and irregularities. And he further understands that these irregularities can be understood or absolved through the good offices of sympathy and compassion. It is this kind of mature love that Moravia delineates in the character of Vagnuzzi. Possessed with intelligence and sensitivity, Vagnuzzi's contempt yields to a deeper thoughtfulness.

> From Elvira's furious remarks and Gemma's replies he had been able to understand very little beyond the main fact. But he realized that it would now be useless—nay worse, ridiculous and actually harmful—to go and seek out Elvira, who had made her escape . . . or, indeed, to question Gemma when she was well again. He pondered for a long time upon what course of action he ought to take. In the end love for his wife was more potent than disappointment or anger, and he made up his mind that the best plan would be . . . never to speak of what had happened. It would be best for him to look upon the Vittoni adventures as a mere youthful error. Later on, in a different town and with a different circle of acquaintances, Gemma and he would in time forget all about it and even think it had never occurred. Perhaps the greatest bitterness was having to give up, for the moment anyhow, all thought of the child he had so longed for. Then, putting aside all further reflections . . . he directed every effort towards his wife's recovery.[33]

This is one of his finest descriptions of a husband's love for his wife. We cannot help but be moved by

Vagnuzzi's devotion and his enormous maturity. The love he holds for Gemma is that which is most dear and real to him, and even the heavy price of wounded narcissism cannot force Vagnuzzi to part with it.

Gemma's illness and delirium, recovery, and the promise of Rome seem to be those outward events which symbolize an even more revolutionary inner change. As the story concludes, we catch a last glimpse of husband and wife on a bus which will take them to Rome and a new life.

This novella gives rise to a host of literary associations. Gemma, poisoned by still another mother, daydreams about the indulgent, luxurious high life she imagines others to have, like a modern Emma Bovary. Gemma, like Emma, is a victim of certain novels and romances which (to quote Chekov who is a master of this twentieth-century *donnée*) flatter us "because they make us think we can behave like wild beasts and still call ourselves happy, amass great wealth and still retain our innocence." She opens her mouth to tell the truth but out comes falseness. In the Chekovian manner (as with Nina) she will suffer and lose her baby before good faith comes. After her affair is over, Gemma sees herself as a worthless reject. Her I and her Me are without distinction, to speak in Sartrean terms; she views herself as an object, as a thing In-Itself. Then there are echoes of Platonic purity as her spirit begins, through suffering, its purgation.

Clearly Moravia tells us that Gemma's break with Elvira is symbolic of a break with her mother and all the "infatuations that had blinded her ever since the years of adolescence." Gemma must rid herself of the mother who first started her on the path of self-delusion. The contempt and disgust which she feels for Elvira is nothing more than that which she feels for the whole of her past life. Gemma's revolt is one against her own mother and the years of falsity which infected her as a child and continued to grow inside her like a terrible disease. When Elvira moves in with Gemma and her husband, Moravia lucidly relates the girl's unconscious suffering.

> During . . . the day she avoided her as much as possible. But . . . she was always present to her. It was like having an ugly festering sore, cold and moist, painless but incurable, under her clothes, a thing she could never manage to forget though at the same time she did not dare uncover it and look at it.[34]

But the disgust of her entire past life can no longer be hidden. Elvira's presence in her home makes this a suffocating reality and Gemma must rebel in order to save herself. In a near-hallucinatory state, Gemma attempts to stab Elvira and thereby purge herself of all past evil. Moravia gives us an interesting insight into the violent passions that precipitate Gemma's act.

> Suddenly a burst of premature maternal jealousy caused her to imagine, absurdly, that Elvira Coceanu would try, by means of yet further blackmail, to take away from her the child that was going to be born. With fantastic but hallucinating clearness she saw her child in the woman's arms, her fat, treacherous, impure face bending over it, while she herself was thrust aside, forced to embrace her child secretly, or when the Rumanian woman allowed her to.[35]

So, indeed, the striking off of memory makes men sick! Gemma remembers (unconsciously with her body), her mother's face. Elvira's face is in reality the impure and treacherous face of her own mother. These echoes of Electra and Clytemnestra reveal Gemma's unconscious fear that her child may be the victim of the same suffocating atmosphere of falsity that plagued her own childhood. She must now save herself *and* her unborn child.

Moravia gives us further psychological evidence of Gemma's revolt against a smothering maternal influence. In her illness she is stricken with fever and delirium. "With rolling eyes and strange words and gestures, she became delirious. She thought she saw a creeping breast, soft and many footed, flattening itself in corners or under the furniture or running rapidly across the floor; and, jumping up in bed to a sitting position, she pointed it out in terror to her husband." [36]

Here is the psyche's fight to the death. To the infant, the breast equals the entire world. The breast (mother-image) is that symbol which carries with it protection, sustenance, love, warmth, comfort, and all things secure. But here, as in *The Conformist* and the story "Mother's Boy," the loving, protective breast has turned bad; it is filled with alienation and bad faith. Camus in *Malentendu* also deals with this most insidious of all evils—crime and bad faith passed on through the symbiosis from a mother to her child—that same evil which fosters Gemma's unconscious terror. It is against this genotype of nihilism that she must rebel.

Moravia pursues the medical metaphor of fevers, poisons, and cures as still another soul runs its course under his gaze. Materiality falls away as Gemma approaches the rim of her inner dialogue. Moravia's insight into human behavior and unconscious motivation is magisterial. His characters' conversions are conveyed with the same masterly insight and subtlety. As husband and wife leave for Rome to begin a new life, Gemma thinks to herself

> In an hour's time . . . Elvira Coceanu will wake up and, her face all greasy and her hair full of curl-papers, will go into the kitchen to make herself a cup of coffee. My mother, too, will begin moving about the house. . . . And the big and little bells in the

churches will start ringing all together for the morning services. But I shall never see Elvira Coceanu again, I shall never again live in the house in the lane, I shall never again hear those bells.[37]

Once again the literary physician has affected a "cure," and we who have witnessed the act of healing emerge the wiser because of it. The final reference is to Moravia himself. Unlike the wife in *A Ghost at Noon*, Gemma lives, but it had only been at the depth of her crisis that her husband had loved her for herself. Not yet a ghost, but hovering between life and death, her existence had manifested itself from his own matrix of need and capacity.

Progression into bad faith first involves, or more likely grows out of, self-deception. As Hazel Barnes observes, bad faith is a particular kind of lie to oneself.[38] It is made up of an uneasy fluctuation between identifying with and disassociating oneself from a situation and conduct. It follows that bad faith infects one's attitude toward himself and his relations with others. Discarding illusion (the painful giving up of narcissism, the ability to look at oneself with complete candor and honesty) is, for Moravia, the heroic deed.

Moravia's Gemma demonstrates the impossibility of an unchanged existence once confronted with a true picture of herself. Once Gemma's past actions become objectified she can no longer retreat into the contentment of self-deception. Or rather she *can*, but she would not emerge as the existential heroine Moravia intended. She has no real choice but to make a new life.

Silvio, too, accepts the truth about himself and is saved. He, like all existential beings, is free to choose what he will be. By choosing to *Be* he refutes the lie about one's freedom. Bad faith is the lie that one is not free to choose what he will be or that he is not responsible for his past actions. But Silvio accepts the "sin" of his bad faith and is saved. This courage in facing his own pretensions and admitting that vanity has corrupted his love, is accomplished with a certain amount of irony. Irony is a persistent staple of the Moravian environment. True to life, solutions to particular problems or reversals of action and thought, while bringing the initial alternation from bad to good faith, do often reveal circumstances of world irony.

Sartre terms bad faith as an attitude of negation against the self.[39] The transition from bad to good faith, from sin to virtue, is not one which can evolve effortlessly or painlessly. The path of sincerity is always the more difficult one and Sartre is the first to admit this. It is precisely this painful changing which makes so few of us real existential men and women. For Moravia this transition is often symbolized by the sickness and pain of delirium and fever. Certainly Gemma's liberating step must be wrested from the pursuing demons of a longstanding psychic malaise. But this association is more than just curious or interesting. In light of the actual pain of life change, this symbol is altogether fitting and appropriate. Self-honesty, abstracted out of physical and psychical crisis, and illuminating the need for change, very naturally brings us to the final and most important thesis of Moravian existentialism. This is the major theme of conversion or life change.

8

Conversion

It is obvious by now that the Moravian world is peopled with a gloomy assortment of unfortunate types—beggars, whores, murderers, thieves, and inverts of every stripe. Furthermore, this literary environment is filled with anxiety, hate, disillusionment, and viciousness; it is sometimes laughable, though rarely funny, and it is most often pathetic and ironic. There are times when even in the hands of a skilled craftsman this world fails to rise above an oppressive bleakness. Surely this is a valid criticism, but it cannot be applied to the entire body of Moravia's work. Though seemingly weighted down by a sordid hopelessness, closer scrutiny reveals that Moravia's vision is balanced by man's salvation.

Salvation—the break with moral nihilism—manifests itself through conversion or life change. It is this conversion, the vital act which places man in "reality," that repeatedly confronts us as we study Moravia in depth. It is the new reality of man, as his life is changed, that one must come to terms with in Moravia's work.

"In a Strange Land," a story from *The Fetish*, is a fine revelation of a young man's disgust with his life and subsequent desire to stop committing those acts which end in futility and desolation. Lucio's visit to a young girl is characterized by unrelieved absurdity. As he enters the apartment Baba announces that she feels out of sorts.

"I warn you, it's a bad day today. I feel strange." [1] Indeed, the girl *is* strange, and this pronouncement sets the tone of the events that follow. Baba begins her bizarre and absurd behavior by playing a 78 record at a 33 speed then she brings Lucio to the window to view a horse defecating outside; next, tries to tear a telephone directory in half.

> It always happened like this, Lucio reflected; Baba started something, then a second thing, then a third, and then got tired in the middle of it, as though she realized the uselessness and absurdity of what she was doing. . . . These were Baba's usual oddities, and for some time now Lucio had lost all curiosity as to why she indulged in them. He felt that there was nothing left for him to do but flirt with her; but it was a feeling of desperation; for, although she attracted him, Baba had for some time past disgusted him with her meaningless eccentricities. [2]

Lucio attempts to kiss the girl but is immediately and violently repulsed and a savage fight ensues. This fight brings with it a violent physical awareness which shocks Lucio. The symbolism here is, of course, that of wrestling with death and madness. Lucio is able to break away. He had begun to see things more clearly as he gazed out the window at the horse. Moravia ingeniously inserts the death symbol in this slightly earlier event. "The wide road below was sprinkled with dead leaves . . . A large transport van . . . was standing on the far side of the road. . . . The doors of the van were open and three men were unloading from it an ugly black chest." [3] It is at this time that Lucio remembers the woodland smell of the rain (the purity of nature) and wonders why he is in Baba's flat.

As the fight discloses the physical awareness of death, he is able to break a smothering relationship with his

desperately bored and neurotic young companion. He
leaves, and Moravia counterbalances Lucio's state of
acute unhappiness with the goodness of nature. Again,
the woodland smell. "Was it possible . . . his life could
never resemble that smell, so good and so alive." It is
then that Lucio admits that he has made a number of
mistakes, but he refuses to be disheartened by this knowledge. "After the mistakes, who knows? he went on to
think, perhaps the right things would emerge." [4]

Though Lucio's change or emergence into a new reality is less dramatic and revolutionary than the protagonists of *The Wayward Wife* and *Luca*, it is nevertheless
as authentic. True, it wavers on the ambiguous, but this
character of ambiguity and uncertainty is an obvious at-
tribute of existential writing, as it is of our existence itself. In his ruthless fidelity to existence, Moravia must
continually depict the ambiguous and inexplicable in
human beings. He just as fiercely defends man's capacity
to change. This change means becoming more real by
the process of knowing oneself, by becoming. Herein lies
the great contradiction, for existential thought does not
admit to the possibility of ever knowing oneself completely. Hence the anxiety and frustration which plague
modern man, for he must continually *try*, he must seek
his own self in spite of this. He dare not turn his back
on the struggle, for it is his only salvation. Existential
literature reveals man seeking this self through endless
introspection and often withdrawal. Though never quite
arriving the courageous self is in a perpetual state of becoming. Lucio's conversion in this story exemplifies the
willingness of a young man to accept the struggle toward
becoming himself. The ancient mythic quest has become
psychic; still in the dark the grail gleams patiently.

The painful process of finding a self through endless
and excruciating introspection is enacted by Dino in
Moravia's most existential work, *The Empty Canvas*.

Dino is bored with external reality and all human relationships. In a desperate effort to form some kind of affinity with the world, he engages in an affair with a young model. This, too, fails to become real for him. Finally Cecilia leaves, and at this point only does she really exist for him. Dino now sees her with new eyes; he now suffers because he cares. This suffering brings on the despair that leads to a suicide attempt. In the hospital Dino reflects on his actions and his, by now, changed feeling for Cecilia. Once again, Moravia uses the sickroom as the setting for bringing his patient back to life, for effecting a conversion.

Dino relates the change in himself as he contemplates a tree outside his window. (Curiously, it was a tree that almost caused his death as his speeding car crashed into it.) In the past, all objects had to have a direct kinship or usefulness for him or they became absurd or ceased to exist. "I now contemplated the tree with infinite complacency, as though to feel it different from myself and independent of me were the only thing that gave me pleasure." [5] He next admits that not only the tree, but any other object would now provide him with the same kind of contemplation and satisfaction. In a final transition Dino views Cecilia in terms of this new feeling.

And indeed, as soon as I began to think about Cecilia again, I was aware of the same thing happening to me as when I gazed at the tree through the window. . . . Cecilia was certainly still at Ponza with Luciani. . . . I knew from experience that happiness is to be found with the person whom one loves and who loves one, in a lovely, peaceful place; I was sure that Cecilia, in her own economical, inexpressive way, was happy, and I was astonished to find that I was pleased. Yes indeed, I was pleased that she would be happy, but above all I was pleased that she should exist . . . in a manner which was her own and which was different from mine and in contrast with mine, with a man who was not myself, far away from me. . . . we were two different people and she had nothing to do with me and I had nothing to do with her. . . . finally I no longer desired to possess her but to watch her live her life, just as she was . . . to contemplate her in the same way that I contemplated the tree. . . . This contemplation would never come to an end for . . . I did not wish the tree, or Cecilia, or any other object outside myself, to become boring to me and consequently, to cease to exist. In reality . . . I had relinquished Cecilia once and for all; and . . . from the very moment of this relinquishment, Cecilia had begun to exist for me.[6]

Dino wonders if in relinquishing Cecilia he has ceased to love her. His former feeling of "love" for her was always delusive and disappointed but he now acknowledges that this feeling is dead.

I loved her all the same, though with a love that was new and different. This new love might or might not be accompanied by a physical relationship, but it did not depend upon it, and in a way did not need it. When Cecilia came back we might or we might not resume our former relations, but I, in any case, would not cease to love her.[7]

Finally, Dino's attitude toward his work, his painting, is changed. Once he is well, he resolves to go back to his studio and try to paint again.

I say that I would try, because I was not at all sure that the connection I had seen for so long between Cecilia and my painting really existed; or that loving Cecilia in a new way would mean starting to paint again. Here again, only experience would be able to provide an answer.[8]

How lifelike Moravia makes this conversion! He never presents a sham idealism that now things will be fine. This passage shakes with uncertainty and the faltering unsureness of a man recuperating from a long illness. In this case the illness is a lifetime of alienation and terrible boredom. At the same time, these final pages extol the joy of discovery, the eagerness to embrace life, the authenticity of a self who resolves to learn from life and not be defeated by it. Bored with being a spectator, Dino now longs to jump into the arena; he is saved through existential commitment! *Amor fati.*

Moravia's most furious attack on the ravages of war is contained in the novel *Two Women.* War brings profound changes to the lives of Cesira and her seventeen-year-old daughter, Rosetta. For lack of food, the two women are forced to leave Rome during the last year of the war. They retreat to a desolate mountain region and for months suffer great hardship. Cesira describes her daughter as an "angel" and is passionately dedicated to protecting her until the end of the war and they can return to Rome.

> It is difficult for me now, after so many things have changed, to explain what Rosetta was like at the time of our flight from Rome. All I can say is that at times I thought she was perfect. She was one of those people whom you cannot find any flaws in even if you are unkind. Rosetta was good, frank, sincere, disinterested. . . . Rosetta never answered me angrily, never nursed any resentment, never showed herself anything but a model daughter. Her perfection, however, did not consist merely in having no defects; it consisted also in the fact that she always did and said the right thing, the one thing in a thousand that *ought* to be done and

said. Very often I felt almost frightened and said to myself: I have a saint for a daughter.[9]

Moravia uses this young girl as the very personification of purity and goodness. Rosetta might also symbolize modern Italy before she was ravished by the Fascists and subjected to the terrors of war. This theme of the corruption of goodness and innocence is the essence of *Woman of Rome* as well. Rosetta is raped by a band of Moroccan soldiers and out of shock and seeming indifference becomes a cheap prostitute. Cesira is horrified at Rosetta's deterioration and at her own transition to a common thief. In order to survive, she herself has resorted to stealing. The conversion in this story is particularly moving and pathetic as it must be extorted from the suffering and despair of two women subjected to the horrors of total war.

As the war ends, Cesira and Rosetta are able to return to Rome. True to his pattern, the author uses this trip to extol his visions of Homer and of Mother Nature, that most ancient of all goddesses. But the despairing Cesira feels that the country has betrayed her and she seems to have no hope left.

It was well on in the morning by this time, and the sunshine was blazing hot and dry, and full of the cheerful strength of youth; the road was white with dust, the hedges also were white with dust, and whenever the truck slowed down you could hear the chirping of thousands of young cicadas hidden amongst the foliage. . . . This was indeed the real country, my own beloved countryside in which I had been born and brought up, and to which I had turned, in the perplexities of famine and war, as one turns to a very ancient mother who has experienced everything and has yet remained kind and good and who knows everything and forgives everything. But the country had betrayed me and everything had ended badly, and now

I myself had changed although the country had remained the same as ever. The sunshine warmed everything except my frozen heart, and the cicadas which
are so lovely to hear when you are young and love life
were now almost annoying because I had no hope
left, and the smell of the dry, hot dust which is in-
toxicating to the senses when they are still virginal
and unsatisfied, now seemed to suffocate me, as
though a stifling hand were placed over my nose and
mouth. The country had betrayed me, and I was going back to Rome in despair, without any hope. I wept
quietly and drank the bitter tears that flowed from my
eyes, trying to keep my head turned away so that Rosario and Rosetta should not see me.[10]

The journey continues and Cesira reflects upon the
dreadful changes war has inflicted. For her, the whole of
life has now become absurd. Mingled with this absurdity
is Cesira's anxiety for Rosetta who she fears has become
indifferent and apathetic, completely without feeling or
pity. The ruined countryside now becomes synonymous
with her own ruined life.

Here were the floods caused by the Germans when
they blew up the dikes, their blue waters, ruffled by
the breeze and broken by tufts of trees and ruins,
spreading far and wide where once there had been
cultivated fields and farms. . . . Soon came Terracina, and it made an even deeper impression upon
me than Fondi—an utter desolation, with all the
houses flayed by machine-gun fire and pitted with
holes, and their windows black like the eyes of blind
people or, worse still, blue, when there was nothing
left but the facade of the house; and mountains of
dusty debris and ditches full of yellow water everywhere. . . . I felt that the same thing must have happened at Terracina as at Fondi: the first day, a kind
of fair ground, a huge crowd, soldiers, peasants and

evacuees, distributions of food and clothes, joy and hubbub—life, in fact. Then the army had moved on toward Rome, and life had vanished and nothing had been left but a desert of ruin and silence. . . . In the ditches at the side of the road you could see the carcass of some military vehicle, its wheels in the air, already rusty and unrecognizable . . . and again, in a cornfield, you could distinguish the long, thin gun of a tank, motionless, pointing at the sky, and, as you came nearer, there was the whole tank submerged beneath the tall ears of corn, still and gaunt like some great animal stricken and left to die.[11]

Like Adriana in *Woman of Rome*, Cesira emerges as one of Moravia's great souls. Subdued by calamity, she tries to kill herself.

There came over me a despair and a frenzy that I cannot describe; I did not wish to live any longer in a world like this, in which good men and honest women had ceased to count for anything and criminals behaved as if they were the masters. With Rosetta in her present state of degradation, life now had no more meaning for me, and even in Rome, with my flat and my shop, I should never be the same as before and should have no further pleasure in living. Suddenly I felt that I wanted to die.[12]

But Cesira possesses a sweetness of spirit and an indomitable will which refuse to be broken by the painful blows of tragic circumstances. Even on the brink of suicide she cannot abandon the life which she sees at last as absurd and meaningless. Cesira's conversion is foretold by the change that overcomes Rosetta on that fateful journey back to Rome.

Then an odd and unexpected thing happened: Rosetta began to sing. At first in a hesitating, strangled sort of voice, then in a voice that became clearer and firmer and more sure of itself, she started to sing the same song that I had asked her to sing not long before. . . . Then I remembered that when I had asked her to sing she hadn't been able to . . . and I had reflected that the reason why she could not sing was that was no longer the same person as before. Now I said to myself that by starting to sing again she perhaps meant me to understand . . . that she was still the Rosetta of former times, good and sweet and innocent as an angel. I looked at her and I saw that her eyes were full of tears. The tears were brimming over from her wide-open eyes and sliding down her cheeks, and all at once I felt completely sure: she was not changed, as I had feared; these tears she was shedding were partly for Rosario, who had been killed without pity, like a dog, and partly for herself and for me and for all those who had been stricken and maimed and destroyed by the war. This meant that not only had she not changed, fundamentally, but that I had not either, although I had stolen Rosario's money, nor had all those whom the war had made like herself, throughout the whole time it lasted. Suddenly I felt comforted, and spontaneously, from the comfort I felt, sprang the thought: "As soon as I get to Rome, I shall return this money to Rosario's mother." Without saying anything I slipped my arm under Rosetta's and clasped her hand in mine.[13]

The dome of St. Peter's comes into view and Cesira is filled with hope and reassured by the familiar, solid surroundings. Mother speaks of "Mother" Rome:

That dome, for me, was not merely Rome, it was my life in Rome, the serenity of days lived at peace with oneself and with others. Far away on the horizon, that dome was saying to me that I could now return home confidently and that, even after so many changes and tragedies, the old life would take up its course again. It also told me that I owed this new-born confidence to Rosetta, and to her singing and her tears. And that, had it not been for this sorrow on Rosetta's part, there would have arrived in Rome, not the two unoffending women who had left it a year before, but the thief and the prostitute which they had become, during the war and because of the war.[14]

Cesira's feelings give way to an immense joy; the joy of being resurrected from the dead. She admits that she and Rosetta had indeed been dead, "dead to the pity that we owe to others and to ourselves." [15] But sorrow has saved them at the last moment. Cesira senses herself emerging from a tomb of indifference and evil, able, once again, to walk along the path of her own life. She admits that this life was perhaps "a poor thing full of obscurities and errors but nevertheless the only life that we ought to live." [16]

Absolute existentialism. They are not the petty bourgeoises who left Rome; they are not the thief and the prostitute; they are two women, beyond mother and daughter. Rape and murder, the limits of identity, have forced them beyond their former roles or their inversions (the words "thief" and "prostitute" depend on the same moral vision being held by judge and prisoner); their identities as human beings are springing from the ruins of their received "personalities." The existential transaction is signaled by the moment of I-Thou when mother clasps daughter's hand spontaneously.

Moravia seems to agree with Sartre's first existential principle, "Man is nothing else but that which he makes of himself." [17] Existentialism further admonishes us that there is no hope except in man's action and that "the one thing which permits him to have life is the dead." [18] If Moravia's characters tell us anything, it is precisely this—that man will be what he makes of himself and he will attain existence when he is what he purposes to be. In *Der Messingkauf*, Brecht hurls the same challenge, "the word has spread that mankind's fate is man alone."

Camus, too, in a slightly different vein, echoes this same lesson that man's fate is his own. "Yes, that's how it is: yes, the world is absurd; no, nothing is to be expected from the gods. And yet, faced with this implacable fate, it is of consequence to acknowledge this fate, scorn it, and, insofar as it is humanly possible, change it." [19] As it is humanly possible, *change* it! This is the positive cry of the Moravian sufferer as he rebels against the absurdity of suicide or moral nihilism. What but senseless suffering and mortality (the absurdity of death) enhances the value of life, inviting man to live it more intensely?

As Moravia's men and women make the commitment to life, "reality" changes for them. Time and time again, they experience a new way of feeling, a new way of looking at the world; they see things in a new light.

In *Luca* and *The Wayward Wife*, conversion must evolve out of sickness bordering on death. Infected from early childhood with the false ambitions of pride and vanity, Gemma travels a long, confused, and bitter road to acts of good faith and conversion. But as with Luca, after illness and its accompanying delirium and fever, the author brings Gemma back to life through existential conversion. Luca is recalled to life by the love and concern of a sympathetic and understanding nurse. The theme of the loving vigil is enacted at Gemma's bedside by her devoted husband.

Luca emerges from his delirium a changed individual. Moravia details this adolescent's conversion with a remarkable vividness and clarity.

Then, as the fog of delirium gradually cleared away . . . he noticed a strange thing which was entirely new. The nurse, . . . the room which he had once hated, every single object, in fact, appeared to him in a new light—serene, clean, familiar, lovable, and so to speak, appetizing. . . . He felt that all these things wished him well; and he seemed to be repaying their goodwill with a corresponding feeling of sympathy.[20]

Delighted with his new vision, Luca continues to observe the nurse, the bottles on the table beside his bed, the various pieces of furniture around the room, and takes pleasure in all of these things.

Everything, in fact, to these new eyes of his, seemed to have significance—a very humble and homely significance, it is true, but a positive one. To the benevolence that colored all reality with fellow feeling there was added . . . the sense of an established order, modest but necessary, in which nothing appeared absurd and devoid of usefulness.[21]

In his uniquely personal style and with astute psychological insight, Moravia gives us a picture of Luca's change toward *himself*. The nurse washes his face, then asks Luca to hold the mirror while she parts his hair. The sight of his own face inspires a profound astonishment.

His face, refined by illness, seemed to have emerged purified from fever and delirium. . . . He was conscious of a feeling of love for that adolescent face which looked back at him, dreamy eyed. It was true that this was the same love that he felt for the nurse and for all the other things; but when he remembered the hatred that he had once felt for himself he saw that it was the most important feature of this new change.[22]

This is not solipsism. This is Being, the For-Itself. This is libido and eros, itself. Luca is aware that since awakening from his delirium, he now derives pleasure from everything that happens, from every presence and every relationship. He also feels himself attracted to the nurse but he does not experience, toward her, any feeling more intense than or different from the feeling inspired in him by other people and all other objects. Luca's experience is the other side of the glass from Sartre's description of the mirror in *Nausea*.

> He [Luca] was, in reality, hungry for this woman, and this hunger made her desirable to him; but the same way he was hungry for the peaceful light shed by the lamp at his bedside, for the pieces of furniture standing in the shadows, for the night, for the silence that he imagined outside the house. . . . These things, and many others . . . because of this hunger that made them appetizing to him, were all equally lovable and together composed a world which was new to him and at last acceptable.[23]

Moravia characterizes the emergence from delirium (conversion) with feelings of appetite and hunger. Again, the metaphor bears a striking fidelity to nature. Certainly the return of appetite after illness is one of the most valid indications of the return to good health. Hungry for life, the world is now acceptable and desirable. This is the end of Luca's frightening alienation, his estrangement from life, his nausea that nearly led to death. After his final recall to life, through sexuality, Luca admits he has now found "a new and quite personal way of looking at reality—a way that was composed of sympathy and patient expectation." [24] Furthermore, Luca understands that this new perception permits a rhythm of thought much calmer, much fuller and much more serene than before. From now on he will see things with "those new eyes which had opened that night inside him." [25] Peter Weiss traces this suffering and conversion closely when he has his character, Jean-Paul Marat, say: "The main thing is to pull yourself up by your own hair, turn yourself inside out and learn to see the whole world with fresh eyes." [26]

Dino's conversion in *The Empty Canvas* bears a certain similarity to Luca's. Dino evidences the same sense of absurdity in relation to external objects that Luca experiences. Recuperating from the near-fatal car accident, Dino contemplates a tree outside his hospital window. The tree, which earlier would have bored him because it had no immediate relationship to him is now viewed with pleasure and satisfaction. He finds that objects can exist outside of himself and still have meaning of their own; they no longer seem absurd. Dino is surprised to find that this new way of "seeing" extends to his personal relationships, specifically to Cecilia. He characterizes this new feeling as love—but a new and different kind of love. Released from the inner compulsion to merely possess Cecilia physically, Dino's love has expanded, it is now free and unselfish. This gratuitous expression of love is apparent as Dino admits, "I had learned to love Cecilia . . . without complications." [27]

Gemma, in *The Wayward Wife*, discards the illusions about herself and her social pretensions and she, too, comes to grips with reality in a new and different way. Confronted with the roughness and sham of a meaningless affair, Gemma is open to an enlightened understanding of the fine qualities of her adoring husband. As her perceptiveness increases, she senses that there is an "ideal world in which the soul likes to see itself reflected as in a piece of smooth water," and the soul cannot be at peace "until it sees this world always clear and transparent." [28] A perfect and impossible Platonism. It is out of this impossibility, of course, that the alienation of relativism and the therapy of existentialism emerge.

In recognizing the theme of conversion in the works

of Moravia it is important to recognize the *totality* of his protagonists' conversion. To be sure, this conversion brings life changes, sometimes drastic ones, but as the preceding passages point out, Moravian conversion entails more than this. Not only does action change but "reality" changes or it is enlarged by certain important ramifications. Conversion brings a new intensity to life, a new way of looking at the world—an increased awareness and responsiveness, not only to external objects but to all human relationships as well. Here the word love must be used. For surely it is a kind of love that Luca speaks of when he recognizes a "benevolence that colors all reality with fellow-feeling." This feeling—this love—permits the converted patient to regard the total world of his experience with compassion and fellowship. All experience is now joined with a perception much calmer, fuller, and more sensuously serene than before. The author reinvests the objects and properties of life with existential subjective meaning. This is a giant step further than that other new novel that, having emptied the world of received mythological meaning, stares at its objects like a computer from Mars.

9

Conclusion

Moravia's portrayal of violence, his sexual candor, his incisive and unsentimental intelligence spring directly from a reaction to the brutality of twentieth-century life. As we recall his long years of childhood illness and convalescence, his fear and hatred of fascism, his eventual exile in the mountains, his sensitivity to the dehumanization of man through two worldwide holocausts, we know that the forces which have shaped Moravia's dark and tragic view of life are very real indeed.

Moravia's identity appears to be that of the radical European. There is abundant example in this century, however, of the merger of a certain Jewish sensibility to suffering with a rational Europeanism. Over all are Marx, Freud, and Einstein. Without these Prometheans there would be no existential vision, no stern questioning of reality. Proust and Kafka, so ambiguous in their national identities, were able to fathom and translate the very questions of the century into their work, and Kafka is, in many ways, the father of the twentieth-century novel just as Joyce's Bloom, a Jew, is the father of the antihero. We may assume the impact on Moravia of Heine, Buber, Bergson, Hofmansthal, Werfel, Ernest Bloch, Wittgenstein, Pasternak, as well as a host of Jewish ideologues of the existential vision. An inheritance evoked by his obsession, the twentieth-century obsession, with the camps and the bomb. Far more important than these modern sources, though, is Moravia's Homeric loyalty. It is here that he, like so many since Aeschylus, have found their models of lucidity and passion. This existentialism, then, rotates on several axes: the classic, the Jewish, the psychoanalytic, and that of linguistic analysis.

Moravia, it is interesting to note, does not at any time fit into that other great tendency of modern literature—Marxism—that takes as its *donnée* that same Western scandal of capitalism and poor people and war and racism. Confronted by a degraded environment, Moravia, in case after case, chooses radical rebellion and intrapsychic confrontation instead of social revolution. He is almost always the therapist feeling his way, rather than the armed intellectual. Too often Moravia follows what Marxist critics call the negative strain of romanticism (meaning, usually, Dostoyevsky), foregoing the positive strain which becomes, all too often, a mindless celebration of dialectical materialism. All this is rapidly changing in Marxist literature now, long after Moravia's tendencies had been grooved for life by the tragic. Tragifarce is a twentieth-century mutant resisting Marxist *tendenz-poésie*; and Moravia, like the Camus of *The Fall* or the Sartre of *Nausea*, dispenses prescriptions of this bitter brew. He goes with the existentialists to the "far side of despair" not with the Marxists to "the other side of history."

First, and foremost, Moravia is a storyteller and human behavior is at the core of his fictional world. Though at times the writing is tedious, a little contrived, or a little too polished, it is always very much alive. At his best, Moravia emerges as a rare cynical genius who illuminates his world with a penetrating psychic understanding. Indeed, his insights are handled with the depth and subtlety of a master psychologist. As his characters reveal their needs; our own necessities are disclosed. To understand Moravia fully is to lose our "intolerance"; he makes us aware, conscious, knowing. We cannot escape facing the challenge to be compassionate and different. In Moravia's work it is always the individual that counts. This is apparent from his own words, "I have at heart, above all, the human person . . . with his name, occupation, age, face, body, arms, legs." [1]

Moravia's view of life emerges as essentially tragic. His great fear is that man has become a machine, an automaton or "thing," more fearful still, a means. "The use of man as a means and not as an end is the root of all evil." [2] He has said, "Man is automatically not to be happy, that is the human situation." However, it is out of this very morbidity, this unflinching courage in portraying man as he is, that Moravia's vision becomes heroic. Faced with the absurdity of life, an absurdity which equals suffering, his characters nevertheless survive. Man can rise above adversity. As the banished, wretched beggar is able to say in "Slave-driver," life is "like a seesaw, all ups and downs . . . nevertheless I don't despair; the seesaw will go up again and I shall go back to Rome." [3] Man does not have to be destroyed by circumstances; he has the inner resources to conquer defeat and avoid destruction. Whatever the horrors, man can survive.

Over and over Moravia uses crime and brutality to illuminate man's absurd condition. Violence and crime make man aware of the other extreme he is capable of through love; hence, a higher existence is revealed. Compassion, that capacity to feel sorrow, solidarity, sympathy —to suffer, not only for your own predicament but for that of others—is the key to Moravian love. To be willing to assume the sorrows of others and to suffer because of (and with) others is the challenge which Moravia would demand us to accept. Instead of the old pity and terror of literature, the existentialists present us with anguish and radical solidarity.

Moravia has gone beyond the bleak, sordid vision of *Time of Indifference*. In subsequent works his perception has deepened and matured. Out of this intense vision we sense a true empathy for the condition of modern man. This growth toward understanding and compassion is that factor which earmarks Moravia's greatness; he has gone beyond the existential nausea of *Time of Indifference* to existential compassion in the later works.

The author has made the statement that, "The writer's task is to perfect the one problem he was born to understand." Certainly, he himself has taken this task seriously. Over and over in his desolate, gloomy, ironic world, the central theme that emerges is the relationship between man and reality. Further, as Moravia's world is a carnal one, his characters most often establish their own reality through a relationship with the opposite sex. As this is accomplished, all other relationships fall into proper perspective. The reality of sex and money takes precedence with Moravia, but with valid reasoning. Giuliano Dego observes,

Money and sex, the two constant poles between which bourgeois and neo-capitalist society move, are then, in the writings of Moravia the only basic criteria for every interpretation of existence . . . the only realities that we cannot reduce farther are sex and money. . . . Within this context Moravia takes up an attitude peculiar to him: he always attacks the character first of all from the outside, almost as if a minute description of the body could indicate in some manner a way of approach to the soul. . . . It is as if in the last resort all the good and evil, or better the chaos that is within, could paradoxically find its expression in a mould, in a corporeal mask.[4]

But Moravia's preoccupation with the sexual motif is not carried to the point of abuse as some critics feel. He, himself, is willing to clarify this motif.

> My concentration on the sexual act, which is one of the most primitive and unalterable motives in our relation to reality, is due precisely to this urgency; and the same can be said of my consideration of the economic factor, which is also primitive and unalterable, in that it is founded on the instinct of self-preservation that man has in common with animals . . . sex in the modern world is synonymous with love. Who can deny that love is a very frequent subject in the literature of all times and all places? But, someone will say, has love been transformed into sex in modern literature . . . has it lost the indirect, metaphorical and idealized character it had in the past, and so ended up by being identified with the sexual act? The reasons for this identification are many; the chief one is the decline in the taboos and prohibitions which too often compelled false idealizations of the erotic act in an artificial way.[5]

In this existential framework of Moravia's, the quartet of love, existence, reality, and suffering are irrevocably joined. They interlock, interrelate, overlap; they are interdependent. Without love man does not really exist— "he is a mere dehumanized item of existence." [6] Existing implies a new perception and enlargement of reality. As the struggle to exist (conversion) defeats the forces of nonexistence, nihilism, and absurdity, everything changes. *All* things are seen in a new way—a new reality emerges. Camus, too, seems to traverse this same path back to life via the absurd and suicide. He would have us jolted from the monotonous pattern of our everyday lives. "It happens that the decor of daily life crumbles . . . one day the Why appears and everything begins in a weariness tinged with surprise." [7] *Everything . . .* tinged with surprise! This can only mean that we begin to look about us with a new style. A new vision is the beginning of *revolt* for Camus, as therapeutic in its consequences as *conversion* is for Moravia.

Moravian reality, as we now understand it, is inextricably linked to love, to compassion: that capacity to feel anguish, solidarity, tenderness, and sympathy. Further, through this love, this compassion, man suffers; not only out of his own predicament but for the predicament of others. He must be willing to assume the sorrows of others—to suffer because of, and with others. This reality is filled with pathos as it is intimately merged with the sense of experience as suffering. It is through love that man suffers. Suffering becomes the contingency of love. Man is exalted through love when he can face this contingency; when he has the courage to commit himself to love even though he knows that this exposes him to the possibility of great suffering. Commitment to love, without the possibility of overlooking the risks, is what makes man, fine, elevated, superior, the overman.

Man establishes the sense of his own identity, his own reality, *becomes* himself in the most profound terms when he loses himself in a love relationship. As man loves, he transcends the banal, the common, the narcissism of everyday existence; he experiences that which is better than himself. His perception of himself, of objects, of nature, of the world around him becomes valid and meaningful. Through love he suffers, and by suffering he can understand, he can know, he can experience, he can feel, he can act—he is alive.

Reality is coeval with love. As man loves he gains the sense of reality. But love is fleeting, this is the paradox.

Man is expelled from the world (reality) through loss of love. He can find ways of loving—never permanently, but he is sustained by the memory of love; hence, exile then return through memory to love.

In *The Woman of Rome*, Adriana confides, "I understand that everything was love, and everything depended on love. One had this love or one didn't have it. And if you had it you loved not only your own lover but also every person and everything. And if you didn't have it, you couldn't love anyone or any thing." [8] It is worth repeating Moravia's own revealing statement about love, "A man who makes himself invulnerable to the pains of love is an indecent character, a swine." [9] True reality for Moravia, then, seems to exist side by side with man's capacity to love.

There is in *Luca* a long dream passage of exquisite nature imagery. This passage might be interpreted as a hymn to the totality of Moravia's life-view. It is, at the same time, a summary of the lyric existential reality.

And he had a curious dream . . . in which he thought he was a tree. Shaped like a tree—black, leafless, rain-soaked, numb with cold—he was standing on the top of a bare, frost-bound hill, stretching out his his arms which were branches and his open fingers which were twigs. An immense landscape extended all round . . . and the whole of this landscape was streaked with snow and darkened by winter mists. The sky, heavy with black, unmoving clouds, was mirrored in the flooded fields, and over all there was a profound silence, as of a dead, timeless world. But far away the sun was rising on the horizon. At first it was only a cold, red globe; then, as it rose gradually into the sky, putting the clouds to flight, it became more and more clear and radiant, and he could feel its heat even through the ice-cold bark. Beneath the rays of the sun a vast movement took place over the whole landscape, as though the woods, and every single tree in them, had shaken off their winter stillness, as though the rivers were swollen with flood-water, the fields fermenting with life, the hills softened and filled with nourishment, like a woman's breasts. All of a sudden a harsh sound—exultant, prolonged, amorous, like the call of a hunting horn—filled the air, breaking that cold silence. And to him it seemed that, starting from his roots deep-sunk in the earth, a wave of joyous hunger spread upward through his trunk; and this, overflowing the casing of bark, burst out through his branches in a thousand green and shining buds. These buds, in their turn, swiftly opened, became leaves, tendrils, boughs. And he felt himself growing, multiplying, pullulating endlessly, in an irresistible, fabulous rush of abundance, in every direction and from every part. All at once he was no longer a tree, but a man, standing upright with his arms raised toward the sun. And, with this sensation of rush and thrusting in his limbs, he awoke. . . .

Then, as he looked round the darkened room and thought about the nurse, it seemed to him that this hunger of his, in an impulse of impatience and voracity, was passing, at one step, beyond the limits of the present time and of the place where he now was, and was rushing forward into the future, both in time and in space. There, in the darkness, he seemed to see, rising to the surface, the life that remained for him to live—the places, the human faces, the movements, the meetings. He had an overwhelming sensation of aggressive freedom, of unlimited exploration, of lightning flashes of vision; as though the future, catching alight and burning in the fire of imagination, had been consumed and discounted in an instant, complete even in its smallest details. He saw that this was his life; and that now it only remained to him to be patient and live it out to the end.[10]

Like a tree, man, too, springs from the earth and is nurtured by it. Man, his arms raised to the sun, is free—he captures that sense of "aggressive freedom" and "unlimited exploration." He may be limited by the bounds of his own imagination, but Moravia sets him free to exploit these bounds. Man must live his life to the fullness of his freedom and his imagination. In reading this dream passage we feel the rush and joy of life pulsating in *our* veins, I-Thou.

Moravia is wholeheartedly committed to the writer's greatest task, that of explaining the condition of man in a chaotic universe. From the very start of his literary career Moravia has always asked the fundamental question—how is man to deal with reality? How is he to conduct himself in a world which has become "dark and unplumbable—worse still, had disappeared"? To that singular problem Moravia addressed himself in his first novel and continues the quest to this day with a deepening understanding of man's predicament. Propelled by this quest he endeavors to give us as complete a picture of man as possible. And always, the cause and cure of problems must be found in man's inner self. As if he were born to write endless variations on one story, his style is persistent. Persistence of style—that is the existential equivalent to the old "character."

Moravia comes to grips with the torments, the pettiness, the emptiness, and the hollowness which plague contemporary humanity. He does feel compassion for man's lot and he has intimate knowledge, through personal deprivation, of man's suffering. And the perceptiveness and penetration with which he delineates man's suffering is a measure of this radical solidarity. He opts, finally, for love, but like the older *Mediterraneans* he knows that Eros, as Hesiod wrote, breaks the bones. He is able to stand this risk. He instructs us that if man is to sustain himself in a brutal society he must do so by love—a total commitment to another human being. Moravia speaks to us of ourselves. He is truthful, he is authentic. Is not authenticity the highest praise we can accord any artist in these times or, for that matter, any man?

Notes

1 – The Argument

1. Malcolm Cowley, ed., *Writers at Work: The Paris Review Interviews* (New York: Viking Press, 1958), p. 141.
2. Alberto Moravia, "About My Novels," *The Twentieth Century*, 1964 (December 1958), 531.
3. Ibid., p. 531.
4. Jean-Paul Sartre, *The Philosophy of Existentialism*, ed. Wade Baskin (New York: Philosophical Library, 1965), p. 33.
5. Jean-Paul Sartre, *Being and Nothingness* (New York: Washington Square Press, 1966), pp. 538–39.
6. Alberto Moravia, *The Red Book and The Great Wall; An Impression of Mao's China*, trans. Ronald Strom (New York: Farrar, Straus and Giroux, 1968), p. 92.
7. Moravia, "About My Novels," p. 530.
8. Alberto Moravia, *Man as an End* (New York: Farrar, Straus and Giroux, 1966), p. 53.
9. *Writers at Work*, p. 221.
10. Sergio Pacifici, *The Modern Italian Novel* (Carbondale, Illinois: Southern Illinois University Press, 1967), p. 5.
11. "One Good Tune," *New Yorker*, 31 (May 7, 1955), 39.

2 – Man out of Love and Nature

1. Italo Svevo, *As a Man Grows Older*, trans. Beryl de Zoete (New York: Bantam Books, 1968), pp. 18–19.

2. Alberto Moravia, *More Roman Tales* (New York: Farrar, Straus and Company, 1963), p. 7.

3. Ibid., p. 14.

4. Ibid., p. 207.

5. Italo Svevo, *Confessions of Zeno*, trans. Beryl de Zoete (New York: Random House, Vintage Books, 1958), p. 357.

6. Alberto Moravia, *The Fetish and Other Stories* (New York: Farrar, Straus and Giroux, 1965) p. 79.

7. Ibid., pp. 84–85.

8. Ibid., p. 85.

9. Ibid., pp. 53–54.

10. Ibid., p. 56.

11. Ibid.

12. Moravia, *More Roman Tales*, p. 158.

13. Moravia, *The Fetish*, p. 7.

14. Ibid., p. 260.

15. Alberto Moravia, *The Lie*, trans. Angus Davidson (New York: Farrar, Straus and Giroux, 1966), p. 252.

16. Alberto Moravia, *Bitter Honeymoon and Other Stories*, trans. Angus Davidson (New York: Farrar, Straus and Cudahy, 1956), p. 130.

17. Ibid., p. 136.

18. Ibid., pp. 160–61.

19. Alberto Moravia, *Two Adolescents*, trans. Angus Davidson (New York: Farrar, Straus and Cudahy, 1956), p. 114.

20. Ibid., pp. 164–65.

21. Ibid., p. 209.

3—Alienation

1. Alberto Moravia, *The Time of Indifference*, trans. Angus Davidson (New York: Farrar, Straus and Young, 1953), p. 5.

2. Ibid.

3. Ibid., p. 6.

4. Ibid., pp. 8–9.

5. Ibid., pp. 41–42.

6. Ibid., pp. 117–19.

7. Alberto Moravia, *Two Adolescents*, trans. Angus Davidson (New York: Farrar, Straus and Cudahy, 1956), p. 116.

8. Ibid., pp. 117–18.

9. Ibid., p. 121.

10. Ibid., p. 122.

11. Ibid., pp. 208–9.

12. Ibid., p. 209.

13. Ibid., p. 210.

14. Ibid., p. 221.

15. Ibid., p. 222.

16. Ibid., p. 234.

17. Ibid., pp. 235, 260–61.

18. Ibid., p. 267.

19. Alberto Moravia, *The Empty Canvas*, trans. Angus Davidson (New York: Farrar, Straus and Cudahy, 1961), p. 8.

20. Ibid., pp. 6–7.

21. Jean-Paul Sartre, *Nausea*, trans. Lloyd Alexander (New York: New Directions, 1964), pp. 172–73.

22. Moravia, *The Empty Canvas*, p. 3.

23. Ibid., p. 4.

4—The Dualism of Moravian Sexuality

1. Tennessee Williams, *A Streetcar Named Desire* (New York: The New American Library, Signet Books, 1947), p. 120.

2. Alberto Moravia, *Two Adolescents*, trans. Angus Davidson (New York: Farrar, Straus and Cudahy, 1956), pp. 199–200.

3. Alberto Moravia, *The Lie*, trans. Angus Davidson (New York: Farrar, Straus and Giroux, 1966), p. 19.

4. Ibid., p. 20.

5. Ibid.

6. Ibid., p. 21.

7. Ibid., p. 22.

8. Ibid., pp. 22–23.

9. Ibid., p. 23.

10. Ibid., p. 24.

11. Alberto Moravia, *The Empty Canvas*, trans. Angus Davidson (New York: Farrar, Straus and Cudahy, 1961), pp. 60–61.

12. Ibid., pp. 99–100.

13. Ibid., pp. 147–48.

14. Ibid., p. 148.

15. Alberto Moravia, *Conjugal Love*, trans. Angus Davidson (New York: Farrar, Straus and Young, 1951), pp. 21–22, 34–35.

16. Moravia, *Two Adolescents*, pp. 260–61.

17. Ibid., pp. 264–65.

18. Ibid., p. 264.

19. Richard W. B. Lewis, *The Picaresque Saint* (New York: Lippincott Co., 1959), p. 50.

20. Alberto Moravia, *The Woman of Rome*, trans. Lydia Holland (New York: The New American Library, Signet Books 1951), p. 285.

21. Alberto Moravia, *Man as an End* (New York: Farrar, Straus and Giroux, 1966), p. 228.

22. Ibid., p. 229.

23. Ibid.

24. Ibid., pp. 229–30.

5—The Absurd

1. Eugene Ionesco, *Rhinoceros and Other Plays*, trans. Derek Prouse (New York: Grove Press, 1960), p. 107.

2. Albert Camus, *The Myth of Sisyphus and Other Essays*, trans. Justin O'Brien (New York: Random House, Vintage Books, 1955), p. 91.

3. Alberto Moravia, *Man As An End* (New York: Farrar, Straus and Giroux, 1966), p. 49.

4. Ibid., p. 9.

5. Ibid., p. 32.

6. Ibid.

7. Ibid., p. 33, 45–46.

8. Ibid., p. 35.

9. Italo Svevo, *Confessions of Zeno*, trans. Beryl de Zoete (New York: Random House, Vintage Books, 1958), p. 398.

10. "Our Man In Rome," *New Yorker*, 40 (April 4, 1964), 35.

11. Alberto Moravia, *More Roman Tales* (New York: Farrar, Straus and Company, 1963), p. 126.

12. Alberto Moravia, *The Fetish and Other Stories* (New York: Farrar, Straus and Giroux, 1965), p. 73.

13. Ibid., pp. 74–75.

14. Ibid., p. 76.

15. Ibid., p. 78.

16. Moravia, *More Roman Tales*, pp. 246–47.

6—Nihilism and Crime

1. Friedrich Nietzsche, *Thus Spake Zarathustra*; trans. Thomas Common (New York: Random House, Modern Library, n.d.), p. 37.

2. Alberto Moravia, *Two Women*, trans. Angus Davidson (New York: Farrar, Straus and Cudahy, 1958), p. 115.

3. Ibid., pp. 275–76.

4. Ibid., p. 320.

5. Ibid., pp. 41–42.

6. Ibid., p. 64.

7. Alberto Moravia, *The Conformist*, trans. Angus Davidson (New York: Farrar, Straus and Young, 1951), pp. 6–7.

8. Ibid., p. 73.

9. Ibid., p. 74.

10. Ibid., p. 111.

11. Alberto Moravia, *More Roman Tales* (New York: Farrar, Straus and Company, 1963), p. 176.

12. Ibid., p. 177.

13. Ibid., p. 179.

14. Ibid., pp. 178–79.

15. Ibid., p. 180.

16. Ibid., p. 181.

17. Ibid.

18. Alberto Moravia, *Roman Tales*, trans. Angus Davidson (New York: Farrar, Straus and Cudahy, 1956), p. 21.

19. Ibid., pp. 22–23.

20. Alberto Moravia, *The Wayward Wife and Other Stories*, trans. Angus Davidson (New York: Farrar, Straus and Cudahy, 1960), p. 15.

21. Moravia, *More Roman Tales*, p. 86.

22. Ibid., p. 89.

23. Ibid., p. 91.

24. Ibid., pp. 92–93.

25. Charles I. Glicksberg, *The Self in Modern Literature* (University Park: Pennsylvania State University Press, 1963), p. xxi.

26. Ibid., p. xx.

7—*Self-Delusion* or *Bad Faith*

1. Alberto Moravia, *Conjugal Love*, trans. Angus Davidson (New York: Farrar, Straus and Young, 1951), p. 14.

2. Ibid., p. 39.

3. Ibid., p. 43.

4. Ibid., pp. 114–15.

5. Ibid., p. 131.

6. Ibid., p. 151.

7. Ibid., p. 154.

8. Ibid., pp. 161–65.

9. Italo Svevo, *As a Man Grows Older*, trans. Beryl de Zoete (New York: Bantam Books, 1968), p. 2.

10. Ibid., p. 1–2.

11. Alberto Moravia, *Ghost at Noon*, trans. Angus Davidson (New York: Farrar, Straus and Young, 1955), p. 1.

12. Ibid., p. 3.

13. Ibid., p. 36.

14. Ibid., pp. 246–47.

15. Albert Camus, *The Rebel*, trans. Anthony Bower (New York: Random House, Vintage Books, 1956), p. 306.

16. Martin Buber, *The Knowledge of Man*, trans. Mau-

rice Friedman and Ronald Gregor Smith (New York: Harper and Row, 1965), p. 118.

17. Martin Buber, *I and Thou*, trans. Ronald Gregor Smith (New York: Harper and Row, 1965), p. 118.

18. Moravia, *Ghost at Noon*, p. 142.

19. Hazel E. Barnes, *An Existentialist Ethics* (New York: Alfred A. Knopf, 1967), p. 323.

20. Alberto Moravia, *The Wayward Wife and Other Stories*, trans. Angus Davidson (New York: Farrar, Straus and Cudahy, 1960), pp. 39–40.

21. Ibid., pp. 57–58.

22. Ibid., p. 77.

23. Ibid., p. 88.

24. Ibid., p. 96.

25. Ibid., pp. 98–99.

26. Ibid., pp. 101–2.

27. Ibid., pp. 105–6.

28. Ibid., p. 103.

29. Ibid., p. 109.

30. Ibid., p. 114.

31. Ibid., p. 116.

32. Ibid., p. 117.

33. Ibid., pp. 118–19.

34. Ibid., p. 113.

35. Ibid., p. 116.

36. Ibid., p. 117.

37. Ibid., p. 119.

38. Barnes, *An Existentialist Ethics*, p. 82.

39. Jean-Paul Sartre, *The Philosophy of Existentialism*, ed. Wade Baskin (New York: Philosophical Library, 1965), p. 148.

8 – Conversion

1. Alberto Moravia, *The Fetish and Other Stories* (New York: Farrar, Straus and Giroux, 1965), p. 80.

2. Ibid., pp. 82–83.

3. Ibid., p. 81.

4. Ibid., p. 85.

5. Alberto Moravia, *The Empty Canvas*, trans. Angus Davidson (New York: Farrar, Straus and Cudahy, 1961), p. 304.

6. Ibid., pp. 304–5.

7. Ibid., p. 306.

8. Ibid.

9. Alberto Moravia, *Two Women*, trans. Angus Davidson (New York: Farrar, Straus and Cudahy, 1958), p. 96.

10. Ibid., p. 328.

11. Ibid., pp. 329–30.

12. Ibid., p. 323.

13. Ibid., pp. 336–37.

14. Ibid., p. 338.

15. Ibid.

16. Ibid., p. 339.

17. Jean-Paul Sartre, *The Philosophy of Existentialism*, ed. Wade Baskin (New York: Philosophical Library, 1965), p. 36.

18. Ibid.

19. André Maurois, *From Proust to Camus*, trans. Carl Morse and Renaud Bruce (New York: Doubleday, 1966), p. 353.

20. Alberto Moravia, *Two Adolescents*, trans. Angus Davidson (New York: Farrar, Straus and Cudahy, 1956), p. 235.

21. Ibid., pp. 236–37.

22. Ibid., pp. 237–38.

23. Ibid., pp. 254–55.

24. Ibid., p. 260.

25. Ibid.

26. Peter Weiss, *The Persecution and Assassination of Jean-Paul Marat as Performed by the Inmates of the Asylum of Charenton Under the Direction of the Marquis de Sade* (New York: Antheneum, 1965), p. 27.

27. Moravia, *The Empty Canvas*, p. 306.

28. Alberto Moravia, *The Wayward Wife and Other Stories*, trans. Angus Davidson (New York: Farrar, Straus and Cudahy, 1960), p. 114.

9—Conclusion

1. Charles J. Rolo, "Alberto Moravia," *Atlantic*, 195 (Feb. 1955), 74.

2. "One Good Tune," *New Yorker*, 31 (May 7, 1955), 39.

3. Alberto Moravia, *More Roman Tales* (New York: Farrar, Straus and Company, 1963), p. 255.

4. Giuliano Dego, *Moravia* (New York: Barnes and Noble, 1967), p. 50.

5. Ibid., p. 49.

6. "One Good Tune," p. 39.

7. Albert Camus, *The Myth of Sisyphus*, trans. Justin O'Brien (New York: Random House, Vintage Books, 1955), p. 10.

8. Alberto Moravia, *The Woman of Rome*, trans. Lydia Holland (New York: New American Library, Signet Books, 1951), p. 230.

9. "One Good Tune," p. 39.

10. Alberto Moravia, *Two Adolescents*, trans. Angus Davidson (New York: Farrar, Straus and Cudahy, 1956), pp. 255–57.

Index